Sam Kerr is an Australian p[...] is known as one of the best strikers to ever play the sport. Throughout her career, Sam has shattered records for club and country, both in Australia and overseas. Known for her speed, skill, tenacity and backflip goal celebrations, Kerr is widely considered one of the best female footballers, and strikers, in the world. She currently plays for Chelsea FC Women, is the captain of the Australian Women's National Soccer Team and is undoubtedly one of Australia's greatest athletes of all time.

MY JOURNEY TO THE WORLD CUP

SAM KERR

SIMON &
SCHUSTER

London · New York · Sydney · Toronto · New Delhi

NOTE TO READERS: In much of the world football is known as soccer, so in some cases local terminology has been used where relevant.

MY JOURNEY TO THE WORLD CUP
First published in Australia in 2023 by
Simon & Schuster (Australia) Pty Limited
Suite 19A, Level 1, Building C, 450 Miller Street, Cammeray, NSW 2062
This export edition published in 2023

10 9 8 7 6 5 4 3 2 1

Sydney New York London Toronto New Delhi
Visit our website at www.simonandschuster.com.au

A catalogue record for this book is available from the National Library of Australia

ISBN: 9781761423680

Cover design: Meng Koach
Cover image: Football Australia (front), IOIO Images/Shutterstock (back)
Typeset by Midland Typesetters, Australia
Printed and bound by CPI Group (UK) Ltd, Croydon, CR0 4YY

MIX
Paper | Supporting responsible forestry
FSC® C171272

'It's only a
crazy dream
until you
do it.'

SAM KERR, 2019

CONTENTS

EARLY DAYS

I was born in Fremantle, Perth, one of the most beautiful places on the planet. Mum and Dad had three children when I came along – Daniel, Madeline and Levi – so I ended up being the fourth and last of Roxanne and Roger Kerr's kids. When I came into the world, my dad worked in a client-servicing role at an electrical accessories firm, and Mum had a lot on her hands with three, now four, kids at home.

I was lucky to have had a very happy childhood in Fremantle. Our house was close to the beach, so my older siblings and I spent a lot of time hanging out there together, almost as much time as we did down at the local footy club. But more on that later.

Family holidays were spent near the water, too. Whenever school holidays rolled around, we'd all bundle ourselves into the family car and drive south to one of the beaches along the coast, or head across to beautiful Rottnest Island, which is still one of my favourite places in the world today.

When I started primary school, I found it difficult to concentrate in class. Unfortunately, I was never that good at focusing on any of the work I was given in the classroom and spent most of my time desperately waiting for the lunch bell to ring so I could go outside and play footy on the oval with the boys. The school oval is where I taught myself how to do backflips. I'd spend all of lunchtime practising, flinging my body up and over in the air, freaking out the teachers and my classmates, until I got it right. For as long as I can remember, I've had an innate desire and need to keep my body in motion as much as possible. I've never been very good at sitting still, which is why I became so interested in any games or activities that involved running, jumping, kicking, or hitting balls from a young age.

As a kid, I loved playing sport. It was my number-one passion. So much so that I didn't have, and wasn't interested in, having any other hobbies. I just wanted to spend all my free time running around, kicking balls, and playing cricket or any other sporting activity that was on offer.

Most of my friends in primary school were the sporty boys, rather than any of the girls, and I was totally fine with that. But when I turned ten and had a birthday party at home, my mum made me invite one girl. She was adamant that it wouldn't just be me and a whole heap of boys at my party. Afterwards, Mum said that she had made a huge mistake by insisting I invite her.

The poor girl ended up sitting in a corner on her own all afternoon, while I ran off to kick a ball around with the boys outside.

As I got older, I began to figure out that I'd been born into a family of athletes, so from the very beginning, it seemed like my future career as a sportsperson had already been mapped out for me. My grandpa was a featherweight boxer in Calcutta, India, and my grandma played basketball. Dad was a professional footballer in both the South Australian and West Australian Football Leagues, as were my uncles Con Regan and Shaun McManus. Another uncle, JJ, was a champion jockey who won the Melbourne Cup in 1966. My big brother Daniel started playing for the West Coast Eagles when I was just seven years old. Clearly, sport was in my blood.

Dad was a bit of a trailblazer in the game of AFL. He was born in Calcutta, India, and came out to Australia when he was nine years old to settle in Fremantle. When Dad arrived here, the game of AFL was totally alien to him. Luckily, he was a quick learner and so, alongside his team, ended up winning his first WAFL premiership at the age of twenty five. All up, Dad played 109 games across two states, but it wasn't an easy path for a young Indian guy in the mostly white, and racially naïve, Australia in the 1980s. My nanna has an AFL record from one of Dad's games and the title is: *'Kerr serves curry'*. For the most part, Dad didn't have to put up with a lot of racism, but there's no doubt that it was tougher back then for dark-skinned players in the league than it is now.

'I think loving AFL footy is something I was born with. My dad played, my brother played, all my family played and where I'm from in Perth is AFL through and through. Football, soccer, any other sport is second to AFL.'

Sam Kerr

'We knew she had something at a very young age . . . Her hand-eye coordination was excellent with any kind of ball, even just playing cricket in the house. And she was ambidextrous.'

ROGER KERR

MY FIRST LOVE

Of all the sports I watched and played as a kid, Aussie Rules football (also called AFL) was always my first love. I could never retain any of the information or facts and figures that I learned in class (especially anything to do with maths), but I could easily reel off dozens of AFL stats at the drop of a hat.

It was the sport that I remember being on television the most when I was growing up, and from the very first time I ever saw a game on TV, I was obsessed. Mum says that from the moment my hands were big enough to hold one, I always had a football in my hands. I'd spend hours snapping it down our long hallway, trying to get it through my parents' open bedroom door, which was a Kerr family thing.

My brother Levi wasn't really into sport, and my sister Maddi wasn't that interested either, so it was my oldest brother Daniel who would always head outside with me for a game of footy or a hit of cricket. One of the games we loved to play was standing about three metres or so away from a bucket and seeing who could handball the footy into it. Also, we were always handballing the footy back and forth to each other around the house, driving everyone crazy. From the very beginning, sport was a competition between the two of us. It was just who we were and what we did.

Daniel played for an AFL team, the West Coast Eagles, from when I was very young, and growing up with a big brother who played professional AFL was awesome. That is definitely one of the reasons that I wanted to play, too. I wanted to be like him. It makes sense, I guess. When Daniel was playing out on the footy field, he was a hero to me. Then he'd come home afterwards and we'd talk about the game, which is when he was just my big brother.

My first sporting hero was an AFL player named Ashley Sampi. He was a young Indigenous guy who played for West Coast Eagles, and he was totally electric out on the field. He used to take these amazing screamers up on people's backs and it was incredible to watch. He'd just take off from the back half and run all the way to the forward fifty. He was such a gun and I loved him. I'd spend hours trying to replicate his famous moves. I'd bounce up and off fitness balls in my house and in the backyard to pluck imaginary marks from the air, all to the roar of imaginary fans, all while my mum worried that I was about to break my neck at any moment. It was just footy, footy, footy, all the time for me.

The only sportswoman role model I had when I was growing up was Cathy Freeman. I loved her so much. She was so fast and strong, and she coped so well with the unbelievable pressure that was put on her. I watched her race in the Sydney 2000 Olympics over and over and over again. It was an amazing moment in sporting history. But other than Cathy, all my sporting role models were male. They were all AFL and cricket players, and back then, those were all men. Thank goodness it's different for young girls today. There are so many fantastic women in sport for girls to look up to and be inspired by now.

The whole Kerr family barracked for the West Coast Eagles, but no one was more obsessed with the team than me . . . apart from Daniel, of course, who actually played for them. As soon as I was old enough, I became a member of the Eagles cheer squad, and went along to every single game they played in Perth. There I would be, right down the front of the stands, waving my banner in my full kit and face paint, screaming my lungs out and cheering them on. When the Eagles lost the AFL Grand Final to the Sydney Swans in 2005, I cried for three whole days.

'Both her and Daniel, from Year One onwards, were completely obsessed with sport. And they were both so good. They did it without even trying.'

Roxanne Kerr

OUR GIRL, SAMANTHA: AN INTERVIEW WITH SAM'S MUM ROXANNE KERR

WERE YOU SPORTY YOURSELF AS A CHILD AND TEENAGER?

Roxanne: Yes, passionately sporty! I grew up in a sporty family and played netball from the time I was eight and didn't retire until I was over fifty. Sam's dad Roger was very sporty, too. He played in the West Australian Football League and at one point we moved to Adelaide for a year when he played for Port Adelaide. He also coached football for twenty years once he retired.

Sam played netball, too, and was very good at it. She started playing with the Fremantle Netball Association (FNA) when she was eight and continued right up until she was twelve. She'd play her netball games on a Saturday morning, and her AFL games on a Sunday morning. She was able to fit it all in because she always wanted to play whatever sport she could whenever she could. In netball she always played the position of centre and one day when she was trying out for one of the combined sides for FNA, she yelled out to me, 'Mum, they're putting me as goal keeper'. I'd been playing down there for so long that I knew everyone, so I went up to one of the officials and asked, 'Why have you got Samantha as goal keeper when she's a centre?' The official said, 'Because when Sam's playing centre, nobody else can get the ball. We have to put her in a position that's as far away as we can so the other kids can have a chance.' It was true, because as centre Sam just took over the court, but they loved her down at Fremantle. She was such a nippy little player.

WHEN DID YOU FIRST REALISE THAT SAM WAS A SPORTY KID?

Roxanne: Straight away. Samantha was really into sport from the age of around three or four. She couldn't really play a sport when she was that age, but she always had a ball in her hand or was out the back kicking a ball around.

WHERE DID YOU AND THE FAMILY GO ON HOLIDAYS WHEN THE KIDS WERE YOUNG?

Roxanne: When you have kids who are really into sport like we did, you don't get to go on many getaways except during the school holidays. But when we did go away, we'd head to Point Peron and Rottnest Island. We loved all the open spaces and beaches, and the kids could ride their bikes everywhere. It was great.

WHAT WAS SAM LIKE AT SCHOOL? DID YOU HAVE TO NAG HER TO DO HOMEWORK AND STUDY?

Roxanne: Sam loved primary school, mainly because it was all about sports carnivals and things like that. But I ended up having to move her around a little during her high school years because she was having a bit of a hard time. It was tough because Samantha was always hanging around with kids who were much older than her. When she first started high school Sam was a very good runner and incredibly sporty, and so spent a lot of time with the Year Twelve kids because they were the ones who were really good at sport, too. At high school she'd missed an average of 100 days of school a year because she was playing with the Matildas during that time. She was hardly ever at school. Samantha ended up at Somerville Baptist College and still has at least fifteen close girlfriends from that school today. Even now, when she comes home, they all get together. On Sam's most recent trip home they all rented a house together for two days. They love going to music festivals together, too, and are all still best mates. It's a great group of friends. Her principal was really good and helped her out a lot. She made sure Sam graduated and did all her subjects, because when Samantha went away on tour, she'd be gone for a month or two. Samantha reckons that she did most of her high school lessons in the office with the principal. She couldn't do her final exams in Year Twelve, but she did graduate. I wanted to make sure she did that so if she ever wanted to go to university, she could. I don't think she ever will, to be honest. It's not her thing, but I thought it was important to have a backup just in case she didn't end up with the career she has now.

WERE YOU EVER WORRIED ABOUT SAM PLAYING WITH OLDER BOYS WHEN SHE WAS PLAYING AFL?

Roxanne: Yes, and that's why she had to finish. Girls weren't allowed to play with the boys after the age of twelve because it was such a rough game. Sam was so small that she was always at the bottom of the pack. Also, half the time her teammates and coaches didn't even know she was a girl. When her dad and coach told her she couldn't play anymore she was devastated. She thought it was absolute rubbish and was really upset. Her cousin Dylan played football and is the same age as Sam, so one day he said to her, 'Do you want to come and play with the boys in a football team?' He knew she'd be able to mix in and keep up with the boys even at that young age. So, she went down to the Western Knights and joined a mixed team there. She wasn't keen on football at all in the beginning and didn't really understand the rules, but she ended up winning the best and fairest award every year after that. I remember her coach would give out the trophy and say, 'This girl is going to captain the Matildas one day.' She was twelve when she started playing football and was still playing netball at the same time, but slowly football took over.

In her first year of playing with the Western Knights, the coach of the Young Matildas came up and asked her to try out for their team, but she said, 'No, thanks,' and walked away. He looked at me and said, 'No one has ever said that to me.' But Samantha just wanted to play the game, and at that time she didn't really know what it was all about. She didn't even know there was a national side. She was twelve when she first went over to Coffs Harbour and played in the state titles, and from that tournament they picked their under 15s national team. The coach told me they'd never picked a twelve-year-old – they couldn't because she was too young – but they would have loved to. The year after that, Samantha got into the national team, and it became very full on from then on.

WHAT WAS YOUR OPINION OF FOOTBALL BEFORE SAM STARTED PLAYING?

Roxanne: Football is so different from AFL. In AFL it's all about scoring hundreds of points while in football, you hardly score any. I didn't know anything about football and I remember going along to the game in Coffs Harbour and asking the coach, 'Why don't you let the players run down the flanks and get the goals? And what is this stupid offside rule?' I had no idea and it just frustrated me to hell. He told me that the offside rule exists because when you had players like Samantha, who could outrun everybody, they would just end up getting goals every five minutes if there was no offside, and that's why the rule was made.

It took me a long time to get into football, but I soon got to know the other mums really well and started enjoying it more. We all did so much travelling together and spent so much time with each other, that we soon started booking places to stay together. We loved the tournaments. I went to Coffs Harbour a few times, and to New Zealand with all the mums, and even now, as Matildas mums, we all still make sure we keep in touch about where we're staying and hang out together, which is really good. So, it wasn't my favourite sport in the beginning, but that was only because we were an AFL family, and football is so different. But I love it now, and know *most* of the rules.

WHAT KINDS OF THINGS DID YOU AND SAM DO TOGETHER WHEN SHE WAS GROWING UP?

Roxanne: We spent lots of time in the car together, going to and from trainings and games, so had lots of talks on our drives. We live in Fremantle, and training was 45 minutes away, so we'd be driving in peak-hour traffic, which took some time. We also went out for lunches together, and to the beach near our house a lot. When she was little, I'd always take her on the bus to watch the Eagles play, and then when Daniel started playing, we'd all go as a family. She loves the footy so much. When she comes home now, we still go to watch footy together. I also now look after her dog Billie, so we take him on long walks together when she's home.

DO YOU HAVE ANY HOBBIES THAT YOU ARE PASSIONATE ABOUT IN YOUR LIFE NOW?

Roxanne: My life is very busy. I walk Sam's dog Billie down the beach every day, both morning and night. Roger and I ride our bikes around where we live, and we have five grandchildren, so I look after them a lot and have them for sleepovers. It's a lovely life. Mainly just family time.

IS IT HARD FOR YOU TO GET AWAY FROM WORK WHEN YOU GO VISIT SAM OVERSEAS? HOW OFTEN WOULD YOU VISIT HER WHEN SHE FIRST STARTED TRAVELLING TO PLAY OVERSEAS? HOW OLD WAS SHE?

Roxanne: It is definitely harder for me to get over to England to see her these days when my life is so busy. The travel is so hard because it's not just like going to Sydney or Melbourne where you can go for a weekend. It's so far. She was living overseas at eighteen and people would say to me, 'How do you cope with her living away and overseas at such a young age?' But it was just what I had to deal with. I went over to the USA at least three or four times when she was living there and when it was time to leave her, Sam would always say, 'Are you going to start crying now or on the plane?' Sometimes, I would literally cry all the way home and the flight attendants would come up and ask if I was okay. I'm a sook. But I love travelling. Samantha reckons I'm the only person who gets excited about going to the airport, even if I'm just dropping someone off. I just love it. Because

I'm always so busy, just sitting on a plane watching a movie and having a few drinks is something I don't do very often, so I'm in heaven when I fly.

HOW DOES SAM COPE WITH STRESS?

Roxanne: Sam doesn't really get stressed, but I think that just talking to her sister Maddi and her kids is probably the best medicine for her. She realises that her life is pretty easy when she sees how hectic her sister's life is with two young boys.

HOW DOES SAM COPE WITH HOMESICKNESS?

Roxanne: Sam always says that her cat Helen has been a godsend while she's been living in London. Having Helen there when she gets home to her apartment has been so nice and definitely helps when she is feeling homesick.

HOW DID SAM FEEL AFTER THE 2020 OLYMPICS?

Roxanne: She was pretty disappointed, but also proud that they ended up getting their best result. It was a hard Olympics to play in, because of Covid and the fact that none of us could be there to support her. But whenever she loses a match, I always send her a text that just says, 'bummer', because what else can you say? She writes back, 'Yeah xxx' because she's obviously devastated. I give her a bit of time and then I always call her the next day.

The quote Sam always says to me, which I love about her is: 'Mum, don't worry about things you can't control.' She always grounds me because I'm a worrier. I have four children, so I'm always worried about this one and that one, but Sam is always reminding me not to worry or panic. She's not a worry wart. Sam's attitude is if you lose a game, don't stress. It's over. That's it, the game is finished, and I love that about her. Samantha knows that it's just sport and that you have no control over it, so just enjoy it. She's always been like that.

HOW IS SAM FEELING IN THE LEAD-UP TO THE WORLD CUP?

Roxanne: She's so excited! She can't wait and is just so happy that it's here in Australia.

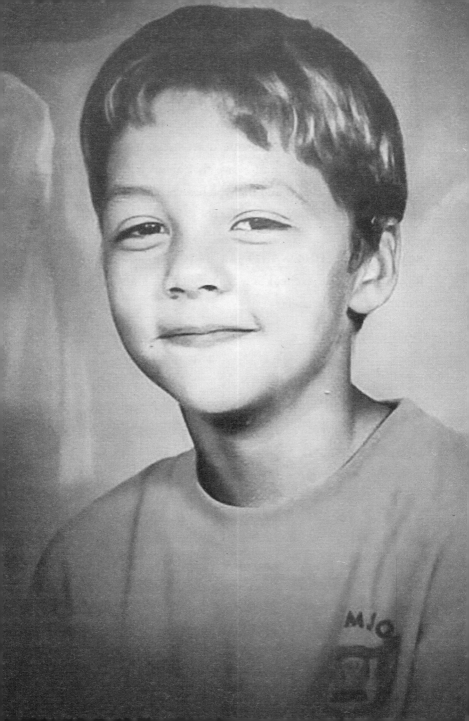

THE AFL KID

Mum and Dad were both stalwarts of the South Freemantle Football Club when I was growing up. Dad also coached the South Fremantle Colts and, for as long as I can remember, he would pick me and my siblings up from school and we'd go straight to the South Freo Club for training. From a young age, spending time at the footy club was as natural to me as sleeping or eating, although in fairness I was a very picky eater when I was a kid . . . it used to drive my poor mum mad. I basically lived at the footy club. During those weekly training sessions and games, I'd run around the oval picking up the balls to hand back to the older boys, watching and listening to everything my dad told his players, and listening in on the meetings in the club. As a result, I learned a lot about the sport at a very early age. My time spent at the South Freo Footy Club was my football education. I loved it, and I certainly learned a lot more there than anything I learned in the classroom at school.

When I was five or six, Dad told me that I was finally old enough to start playing in one of the boys' teams. I was so excited and so very ready. I'd been waiting to get out on the field and play alongside other teammates for what seemed like forever. By that time, I'd been watching the boys play for so long, and had been chomping at the bit to get out there and have a go myself. I knew I'd be the only girl on the team but that didn't worry me at all. When I rocked up to that first training session, the coach me put into the forward position because he said I was a strong player with good hand-eye coordination. Everyone on my team just assumed I was a boy because I had short hair and blonde tips, and I was okay with that. I decided to keep my gender a secret because I didn't want them to treat me any differently just because I was a girl. I loved playing on that team with the boys, and it took a full three years before anyone figured out that I was actually a girl. I still remember one of the boys crying when he found out. But I always got so frustrated when I started playing Auskick because I was told I had to stay in my area. I didn't like that and got really angry because I just wanted to run all over the field. Even now, some of the boys I used to play with come up to me and remind me that I used to run rings around them when we were kids, which I think is really funny but nice, too.

But as good as I was out on the field, and as much as I loved playing the game, the physical differences between the guys and

'Being taken away from footy really sucked and I hated soccer when I was a kid. I never had a soccer ball around the house.'

SAM KERR

me eventually became too pronounced, and the play was too rough. Once we all turned eleven, the boys in my team started growing fast, and soon became much bigger and stronger than me. I was still tiny, so in the first half of that season, they were my size, but by the second half, they were huge. One day, I came home from a game with yet another black eye and bloody lip, and that's when my dad and brother both said, 'Nup, this isn't happening anymore.'

I was getting battered around so much out on the field that it was getting to be a big problem. Dad and my coach both sat me down then and said it was getting far too dangerous for me to continue to play. They said they were sorry, but that I wasn't allowed to play football anymore. I understood the reasons why, but I was heartbroken. Back then, there were no girls' teams in my area for me to join, and to know that I'd never play a sport that I loved so much ever again was devastating.

'I don't even know how to explain it, I just can't imagine my life without AFL footy. Even now, living overseas, I get up in the middle of the night to watch the games, and still know all the players in the league. People in England are diehard football fans, and people in America are diehard NFL fans. I'm a diehard AFL fan, but when I played as a kid, there were no girls' leagues. So, I only played with boys.'

Sam Kerr

'Dreams weigh
nothing.'

SAM KERR

THE EVOLUTION OF WOMEN'S AFL

- **1859:** the first Aussie Rules football game is played by men in Melbourne.

- **1862:** Australian women publicly question why they are not able to play AFL.

- **1880:** a group responding to a postcard from an anonymous 'Lover of Football' gather at Sandhurst, Bendigo, to form an all-ladies football club. This generates attention but ultimately doesn't succeed.

- **1886:** a local newspaper reports sighting a group of women playing kick-to-kick in Williamstown, Victoria.

- **1887:** a group of young ladies participate in a costume football match at the Eastern Oval, Ballarat.

- **1892:** a Bendigo woman is charged with nuisance for kicking a football in the street.

- **1894:** female celebrities of the time participate in a charity football match at East Melbourne Cricket Ground, attracting one of the largest crowds ever seen there.

- **1915:** in Perth, a women's football team made up of department store staff play a match on Perth Oval.

- **1910s & 1920s:** various women play on and off in what becomes known as the shopgirl's competition.

- **1921:** the first match is played in St Kilda, Melbourne, showing that women can play what had previously been considered a man's sport. The umpire wears a skirt.

Women wear kits donated by the St Kilda men's club and shorts rather than dresses. They practise on Saturday mornings at the St Kilda Cricket Ground.

- **1922:** a Fitzroy female team travel to Perth to play West Perth in front of 13,500 spectators.
- **1923:** Richmond ladies football team play against the men's side in Melbourne to raise funds for a junior team's trip.
- **1929:** a thirty-minute charity match is played on the Adelaide Oval between factory workers.
- **1931:** women in Melbourne protest against all-female matches.
- **1941:** a women's football match is played in Tasmania.
- **1947:** calls are made for big VFL clubs to field women's sides.
- **1947:** a round robin all-female competition is played at Glenferrie Oval, featuring the VFL clubs South Melbourne, Footscray, Hawthorn and St Kilda. The league competes through the 1950s and is actively promoted by Ted Whitten and Jack Collins.
- **1953:** the South Fremantle women's side take on and defeat Boans Limited at Perth Oval.
- **1959:** the Victorian squad plays the Tasmanian team.
- **1967:** a charity match is played in Regent's Park, London, between the Aussie Girls and the Wild Colonial Girls to promote the men's match.

- **1981:** the Victorian Women's Football League is formed with four teams competing at open level.
- **1988:** the West Australian Women's Football League is formed.
- **1991:** the South Australian Women's Football League is formed.
- **1992:** the first National Junior Championships for girls is formed.
- **2000:** the number of registered women's football teams increases by 450%.
- **2007:** a mixed gender exhibition match is held in Victoria, raising the profile of women's football in Victoria.
- **2008:** the first AFL Women's Under 18 Championships is held.
- **2015:** 163 new teams are formed in Women's Australian Rules football and a total of 284,501 players take part in organised games.
- **2019:** the AFLW Grand Final in Adelaide sets the record for a stand-alone women's sports fixture in Australia and a new world record attendance for Women's Australian Rules football of 53,034.
- **2022:** a record crowd for AFLW at North Sydney Oval with 8264 in attendance.

'My advice to any young girls playing football is to stay with the boys as long as you can. A twelve-year-old boy is always going to be faster, quicker and stronger. It's a totally different game and it requires more from you. I see young girls who train with us, and I say to them, "You think you're working hard, but you've got to give ten times more." They've been playing with other girls the same age as them their whole lives.'

Sam Kerr

MY SISTER SAM: AN INTERVIEW WITH SAM'S SISTER, MADDI

WERE YOU AND SAM CLOSE WHEN YOU WERE GROWING UP, AND IF SO, WHAT KINDS OF THINGS DID YOU ENJOY DOING TOGETHER?

Maddi: Growing up, Sam and I actually weren't that close, mainly because there was such a big age gap between us – four and a half years – and also because we were very different. Sam was a young kid who was really into sport, whereas I wasn't as into sport as she was. I was also pretty mature for my age. Even when I was just thirteen, I felt and acted much older than I was. I met my now husband when I was thirteen, and we're still together, so I always felt much older than Sam. We didn't fight, but we did have very different interests, which I think made the age gap feel even bigger. But as we got older that started to change. When Sam was fifteen and in high school and started going away a lot with football, we started getting much closer. We'd talk on the phone a lot when she was away, and then when she was home, we spent a lot of time together as a family because we knew she was going away again.

The two of us shared a room up until Sam was about 8 or 9 years old, and we used to play all the normal games like 'Libraries' or 'Mums and Dads', but I would force her to play those games because she didn't really want to. The deal was she would play my games but then I'd have to play her sporty games afterwards. My cousin Alice was the same age as me, and we would make Sam do dances with us to songs by bands such as the Spice Girls. I was very serious doing this but neither of them were taking it seriously, which used to drive me insane. So, we did all of those normal sister kinds of things. But as close as we are now, we definitely weren't like that as kids.

WHAT DO YOU DO NOW FOR A LIVING?

Maddi: I'm a primary school teacher. I have always loved teaching. I teach Grade Two and it's my first year back after having kids (Sonny, 3 and Fraser, 18 months) so it's more of a juggle now, but I still love it.

WERE YOU AS INTERESTED IN SPORT AS SAM WAS?

Maddi: I played netball, as did Sam, at the same club where Mum played and she coached both my team and Sam's team. Mum and Dad would bribe Sam to play netball, telling her she had to play if she wanted to play AFL as well. I love netball and still play it now.

WHEN SAM STARTED PLAYING AFL FOOTBALL AS A KID, DID YOU GO TO WATCH HER GAMES WITH THE FAMILY?

Maddi: I watched Sam's games every weekend. Mum is a life member at the footy club and ran the canteen every weekend, and Dad coached there. Both my brothers played there, too, so we were always at the club and watched each other play.

WERE YOU PART OF THE WEST COAST EAGLES CHEER SQUAD WITH SAM?

Maddi: No, definitely not. That's one place where our differences would really come out. I wanted to sit in the stands and not get wet, while Sam didn't care. She'd be down the front, singing and screaming, but I was at an age where I thought it was just really embarrassing to cheer and carry on like that.

DID YOU EVER HAVE ANY INTEREST IN FOOTBALL BEFORE SAM STARTED PLAYING?

Maddi: No, not at all. I didn't know anything about football and thought it was boring. All of us in the family would go along to watch Sam play football in the beginning to support her, but we didn't understand the rules or know what was going on. Now, of course, it's very different. We love football and watch games that she's not even in, like the men's matches.

DO YOU LIKE TRAVEL YOURSELF OR ARE YOU MORE OF A HOMEBODY?

Maddi: I love travelling and did heaps of it before having kids. I went to South America, Cuba and Asia, and we did heaps of travel with Sam's football – any World Cup or Olympics. When Sam lived in the States, Mum and I went over there a lot. Sam turns thirty this year, so we'll go over to England for that.

DID SAM'S OBSESSION WITH SPORT AND KICKING BALLS ALL OVER THE PLACE EVER ANNOY YOU WHEN YOU WERE KIDS?

Maddi: Not really, because that kind of thing was normal for me. Before Sam, I had my two brothers and my dad doing it all the time, so I was used to it. It only annoyed me when I wasn't playing with Sam and she'd kick the ball directly at me to make me play with her, but otherwise it was just the way it was in my house with balls flying everywhere. Generally, I was made wicket keeper or something like that by Sam and my brothers. They'd always give me some job to do in the game.

My memory of Sam as a kid is that she is still the same person she is now. A giggler, a practical joker and very chilled. She hasn't changed. Sam still has the same personality she had then. With Sam, what you see is what you get. When people ask me what she's like, I tell them that when you see her being interviewed on TV, that's who she is. She's not pretending to be anyone else, which is I think why people like her so much.

DO YOU KEEP IN TOUCH WITH SAM MUCH WHEN SHE'S OVERSEAS?

Maddi: We FaceTime every day. If we don't, then it's like, 'Oh my gosh, what's gone wrong?' Usually, we FaceTime when I'm cooking dinner, or my husband and I are getting the boys ready for bed, which is when Sam is making breakfast and driving to training. The boys take the phone and show her things around the house or in their room, and she shows them her cat Helen, who they love. The time difference makes it hard and it's a bad time for me to be on the phone, but I don't need to entertain her because she's watching the boys play in the bath while they talk to her or play peekaboo. One of my boys will take the phone and talk to her, while I do something with the other one, which is great. And if she's going out to get coffee, she'll show them what London looks like. They love that, too.

WHEN SAM IS HOME, WHAT SORT OF THINGS DO YOU DO TOGETHER?

Maddi: We hang out a lot. When Sam was back for six weeks in June 2022, she'd go to training in the morning and then come over in the afternoon and sit with me while my boys were asleep. We'd chill out together, and then when the kids woke up, Sam would play with them. She'd kick the ball around with them, jump on the trampoline, play cricket, stuff like that. She came over every day, and then every afternoon at around 3pm, she'd say, 'Okay, I've had enough of you guys now,' and she'd leave and go and do her own thing. When she was with us, she'd watch me and say, 'How do you just let them touch your clothes?' or 'All you do is stand in the kitchen and make snacks all day.' Mind you, I'd be doing the same thing for her, making her toasted sandwiches and snacks. I'd say, 'Having you here is like having another kid!'

WHAT TYPE OF AUNTY IS SAM?

Maddi: Sam is the aunty who buys my kids things such as Nerf guns and she even bought Sonny a Thor hammer. I said, 'He's three!' When you don't have kids, buying toys like that for other people's children is fun. Sam would be shooting Sonny with the Nerf gun, and he was shooting her back, and they were both loving it, but when she left, it was his poor little brother who was copping it. Sam's great with the kids and because she misses them so much and has missed such a big part of them growing up, when she's home she doesn't really want to do anything or go anywhere. We go to the beach a lot, and every now and then we might go out to a restaurant for dinner and get a babysitter for the boys, but very rarely because Sam literally just wants to stay at home.

We do very normal things during the day. We don't want to go shopping or do anything like that. We just stay at home or go to the park. It's really nice, especially because Sam usually only comes home for about ten days at a time, which is when we all end up suffocating each other – trying to fit everything in.

But because her visit in 2022 was so long, she still trained and did her own thing every day and would then come over to hang with us after. She came home at Christmas, too, but only for ten days. She brought her partner Kristie this time, which was really nice. We went to Rottnest Island for the day and took Kristie around Fremantle to show her the sights. She is lovely. The two of them would go to training and then come over during the day for lunch, then do their own thing at night while the boys were asleep.

IT BEGINS

Around the time I had to give up football, my cousin was playing football with a local team. My mum and dad could see how upset I was about not playing AFL anymore, so they told me I could go and play football with him instead. I couldn't have been less interested. I was an AFL girl through and through, and didn't know a thing about football. The rules were strange and completely foreign to me. Also, I didn't like the idea of not being able to pick the ball up with my hands and kick it. In the end, I went along to a trial session at a local club, the Western Knights in Mosman Park, just to give it a go.

I was twelve years old when I started training with the Western Knights Junior mixed team, and instantly decided that I did not like or enjoy this new sport at all. You needed completely different skills to play football compared to playing AFL and it was also a lot harder. Suddenly, I was expected to use both of my feet to kick the ball instead of just one, and even though I was an ambidextrous girl, I found it much more difficult to use my left foot. From the very beginning, I could see that this new sport was going to be a challenging one for me to play, but I was determined not to give up before I'd become as good as I could be.

Unfortunately, I was totally crap in my first season with my new team. I didn't know anything about rules such as offside and found it really hard to get my head around them. Out on the pitch, I couldn't understand why none of my teammates would pass me the ball. Looking back now, I can see that it was because they could tell I didn't have a clue what I was doing and wasn't across all the rules. Over the course of that first season with the Western Knights, I only scored three goals. To make things worse, our team didn't win a single game.

It was a huge adjustment for me mentally to go from being the confident, skilled and popular player I had been on my AFL team, to a total newbie who was clueless about the game I was playing. Going from the top of your game, as much as you can be when you're a kid, to the bottom was hard, and I had to face the fact that when it came to this new sport, I was woeful.

To make matters worse, my family didn't like football. They didn't understand the rules, and thought it was a boring, low-scoring game. As a result, they weren't always keen to come and watch me play, which used to frustrate me a lot and definitely contributed to my lack of love for the game of football in the beginning.

Sam was born into a sporty family. Her father, uncles and brother were all professional footballers.

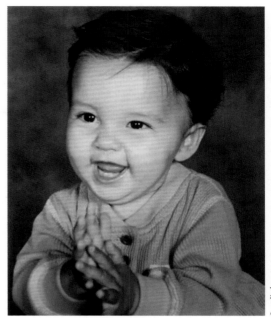

The Kerr kids (clockwise from left): Madeline, Daniel, Levi and Samantha.

Portrait of a young Sam.

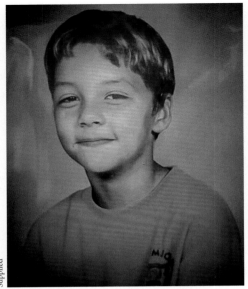

Sam loved playing AFL as a kid but her parents stopped her playing after she starting coming home with black eyes and a bloodied face.

Young Sam winning a medal after her switch to football.

Sam with her beloved dog Indi.

The Kerr family: Sam (left), Madeline (front row, second left), dad Roger (back row, left), brother Daniel (back row, middle), mum Roxanne (front row, right).

Sam has been life-long friends with her Matildas teammate Emily van Egmond.

Sam was soon recognised as a football prodigy after making the switch from AFL.

Sam playing at the West National Training Centre for female football players.

Sam made her debut for Perth Glory at age 15 during the W-League season.

Mucking around with life-long friends Caitlin Foord and Emily van Egmond in 2013.

The Kerr kids (from left): Levi, Madeline and her husband Pascal Kuhn, Samantha and Daniel (with daughter Lola).

Sam with her sister Madeline.

Sam has a special bond with her siblings.

Sam's family are her biggest fans (from left to right): dad Roger, sister Madeline, mum Roxanne, Sam, brother Daniel and grandmother Coral.

Clearly, making the transition from Aussie Rules to football was going to be a struggle, but I was a stubborn kid, and wasn't prepared to give up that easily. I kept working on my skills, determined to get the hang of this new sport and all its strange rules. Figuring out how to use both of my feet in the game was definitely the biggest challenge. It got me down at times, but everything changed when I started scoring more and more goals during matches. Getting that ball past the keeper and into the back of the net gave me such a huge rush of joy and adrenaline. Scoring in football is very different from scoring in AFL. In Aussie Rules, goals are scored much more frequently throughout the game, whereas scoring in football is much harder because of the keeper. Football is a game where everyone can feel the excitement and anticipation building as the match goes on, waiting for that moment when someone scores a goal. When that finally happens, it's a real celebration and a huge high, especially if you're the one who kicked it into the net.

I learned so much from my Western Knights coaches and teammates over that time, and feel lucky to have had the chance to play at such a great club. To this day, I'm so grateful for everything they taught me. The boys in my Under 13s team accepted me as one of their own when I joined, and gave me so much advice, support and encouragement, which made me feel comfortable and secure enough to be myself as I tried to learn the rules of football, a game I was starting to fall in love with.

'Just because you love one sport so much, like I did with AFL, that doesn't mean you can't grow to love and appreciate a totally different sport, like football. Each game has its own unique qualities and things to love.'

SAM KERR

AFL VS FOOTBALL

- BALL
  Football: round
  AFL: oval

- TACKLING
  Football: generally not allowed. No pulling or dragging the opposition to the ground. You can use your body to obstruct the motion of a player with the ball only.
  AFL: allowed. Players may tackle hard between the shoulders and knees, below the knees or charge another player using their shoulder. No contact with the head.

- HISTORY
  Football: dates back to medieval times but was only formalised in 1963.
  AFL: started and was formalised in the 1850s.

- TEAMS
  Football: 11 on field, up to 10 in reserve
  AFL: 18 on field, 4 on bench

- SCORING
  Football: 2–3 goals per game on average
  AFL: 10 goals per game on average

- **FIELD**
  Football: 120 m long and rectangular
  AFL: 135 m long and oval

- **GOAL VALUE**
  Football: 1 point
  AFL: 6 points

- **DIFFICULTY LEVEL**
  AFL is considered more difficult than football in terms of rules to remember and the intensity of play. AFL is a faster game than football, due to the way and speed with which players move the ball up and down the field to score goals.

'I don't like how much football stops. I much prefer the free-flowing game of AFL. I love how football is global, but AFL is restricted to Australia. I still get up in the middle of the night to watch AFL matches, wherever I am in the world.'

SAM KERR

SAM'S BASIC FOOTBALL RULES

For anyone out there who has just started playing football, or who is thinking about starting football, here are my basic rules for playing the game. These are the same rules I tried to learn and remember when I was starting out.

NUMBER 1: DON'T EVER USE YOUR HANDS IN THE GAME

In football, you are never allowed to use your hands during play, unless you're the goalie or if you are doing a throw-in from the sidelines. 'Hands' refers to anywhere from your fingers all the way up your arms to your shoulders.

NUMBER 2: THROW-INS

If the ball goes over the sideline and out of bounds, the throw-in is taken by a player on the team who didn't kick it out. The team member needs to plant both feet on the ground, raise the ball over their head and use both hands to throw it straight overhead and back into play.

NUMBER 3: GOAL AND CORNER KICKS

If the ball is kicked out of bounds behind the goal line by the offensive team, the defensive team takes a goal kick from inside the goal box. If it's the defensive team who kicks it out, then the offensive team takes a corner kick from the corner nearest to where the ball left the field.

NUMBER 4: OFFSIDE RULE

This is a tricky one, but once you get the hang of it, it makes perfect sense! The offside rule means that when an attacking player is in their opposition's half of the pitch, there have to be at least two opposition players, including the goalie, between them and the opposition's goal when a pass is being played out. Basically, no part of a player's head, body or feet can be in the opponents' half or closer to the opponents' goal line than both the ball and the second-last opponent.

NUMBER 5: FOULS

A foul happens if a player kicks, trips, jumps at, charges, strikes, pushes or holds their opponent. If they do any of these things, the team who the foul is against gets a free kick from the spot where they were fouled.

'It is all about doing what I love. I'm relaxed and enjoy what I'm doing, and when the goals come you have more fun. It's a ripple effect.'

SAM KERR

PERTH GLORY

After I'd been playing with the Western Knights for a year or so, a talent scout came along to watch a match that I was playing in. He approached me after the game and invited me to come and trial for the Western Australian State team, Perth Glory. I was shocked but also very excited, and so went along to the trials to see if I could make the team. I played well in the trials and soon after that, in 2008, was offered a spot in Perth Glory, who play in Australia's highest division of professional women's football.

I started in all ten matches during the 2010–2011 season and scored three goals overall. My football journey had officially begun.

THE DREAM DEAL

I had been playing with Perth Glory for a few months when I was asked to join the youth squad for the Matildas – the Australian women's national football team. Obviously, I was absolutely stoked to be making my national team debut at just fifteen years old, but I was also very nervous. Three other young players were chosen for the national youth team at the same time. Those players were Stephanie Catley, Emily van Egmond and Caitlin Foord. I couldn't believe how lucky I was to be in a team with these talented and amazing sportswomen. Stephanie, Emily and Caitlin were all fast, aggressive and physically fearless players, just like I was, and together we made things happen. I'd like to think that we are all still the same kind of players to this day.

But even though I was starting to have all this success with football, I still wasn't feeling much passion for the game itself. I was still an AFL girl through and through. As much as I tried,

I just couldn't find the same love for the round-ball game as I had for the oval-shaped one, so I told myself that I'd keep playing football and do my best for a few more years, then retire when I was twenty-one. Looking back now, I realise how insane that was, but that was always my plan when I was a kid – just do it until I couldn't anymore and then walk away.

I played a few matches with the youth teams, and then at the start of 2009, I was invited to join the Matildas senior team to play a friendly match against Italy. It was my first cap and a massive honour. Although I was excited to be joining the team, I assumed I would most likely be spending the duration of the game sitting on the bench, so I told my family not to bother coming along.

It was February 2009 when I headed off to Canberra with the rest of the senior team to make my debut with the Matildas. It was a surreal, but thrilling experience. As I had expected, my boots didn't hit the pitch for the first two-thirds of the game, but then, in the seventy-sixth minute, the coach told me to get ready because I was going on as a substitute. This was a huge moment for me, and even though my nervousness went into overdrive, I felt that I was ready for this opportunity and was determined to make the most of it. I headed out onto the pitch and gave those last few minutes of the game my all. Even though I didn't score any goals or do anything of any note in that first cap, and although we lost 5–1, that game was a life-changing match for me. Afterwards, I knew that I wanted to play football for as long as I was able, and any thoughts about retiring at twenty-one went out the window. My one regret about that game, my debut with the senior Matildas, was not inviting my family. The Kerr family never saw my first cap and that's a regret I still have to this day.

When the 2009 W-League awards rolled around, I was shocked and humbled to be voted Players' Player. But I was even more stunned when I picked up the Goal of the Year prize for a long-range strike I made in a match against Sydney FC. The biggest buzz came a year later, however, when I helped the Matildas secure their first-ever Asian Cup title in the 2010 AFC Women's Asian Cup. I couldn't believe it when I scored the opening goal in our match against North Korea in the final – my first ever in an international game. We ended up taking out the title via a penalty shoot-out later in the game, and it was my first experience with an international trophy. What an amazing feeling. From that point on, I was officially a round-ball game convert, and all in with this new sport of mine – heart and soul.

'She got the ball in her own half and ran with it for about 70 metres before scoring a goal for Western Australia against Queensland. It's abnormal that a person can run the ball that far at 13 years of age against 15- and 16-year-olds who are the best in their state. Her speed and mobility are the best in the world, and her awareness of space and how to use it are extraordinary and very instinctual. Her hand-eye coordination was excellent with any kind of ball, even just playing cricket in the house. And she was ambidextrous.'

Matildas coach Alen Stajcic
on the first time he saw Sam play

EVERYTHING YOU EVER WANTED TO KNOW ABOUT THE MATILDAS

HISTORY

- The Australian Women's Soccer Association (AWSA) was founded in 1974.

- A national team made up primarily of players from New South Wales and Western Australia was sent to the 1978 inaugural World Women's Invitational Tournament in Taiwan.

- Australia's first official international match was against New Zealand in 1979.

- The nickname for the Australian women's national football team, 'the Matildas', comes from the Australian folk song, 'Waltzing Matilda'.

- When the name Matildas was chosen by popular vote through the Special Broadcasting Service (SBS), the players themselves did not approve of the name, and it took years to use the moniker to describe the team.

- Before 1995, the Matildas were known as the 'Female Socceroos', a derivative of the male squad.

- In 1999, the Matildas had to train with second-hand equipment from the Socceroos. They were not getting paid and only had a few games lined up to play. In an effort to promote themselves and raise funds for the team, the players posed nude for a calendar, which sold more than 40,000 units.

COACHES AND PLAYERS

- The Matildas have had 16 coaches since they formed in 1978, including Jim Selby, John Reid, Alen Stajcic and currently, Tony Gustavsson.
- The longest serving captain of the team to date is Cheryl Salisbury, who led the Matildas from 2003 to 2009.
- The player who has the most international caps is Clare Polkinghorne with 154 games.
- The highest international goalscorer is Cheryl Salisbury, who scored 151 goals between 1994 and 2009. Lisa De Vanna is a close second with 150 goals between 2004 and now.
- Sam Kerr is the Matildas all-time leading goalscorer with 62 goals.

WOMEN IN FOOTBALL: AN INTERVIEW WITH JOHN DIDULICA, DIRECTOR OF FOOTBALL AT MELBOURNE VICTORY

CAN YOU DESCRIBE WHAT IS HAPPENING WITH FEMALE FOOTBALL IN AUSTRALIA?

John: There is an incredible optimism surrounding female football in Australia right now, given how deeply the Matildas have embedded themselves as a totem for what we love about Australia. Those who share this passion appreciate that, in the absence of action that can keep us at the global forefront of female football, this optimism quickly evaporates. The football world is immense – and most nations have now woken up to the social and commercial power of women's football. To keep ahead of that pack will be an immense challenge.

WHAT DOES PLAYING FOOTBALL OFFER GIRLS AND WOMEN?

John: In addition to being a joy to play, football continues to offer girls and women unmatched life opportunities. It offers access to incredible educational opportunities (through the US college system) and is a passport to experience the world – from South America to Asia to Europe to Africa. Its scale as an industry is unmatched. The huge and ever-increasing numbers of girls who are playing football is testament to this.

WHAT MAKES FEMALE FOOTBALL SO SPECIAL?

John: We must be careful to remember what has made female football so special in Australia. It is that close and deep connection with community and celebrating them as people. As we professionalise and increasingly commodify sport, this ethos is often lost.

Sam Kerr is a person of action and authenticity, which is what has endeared her to so many. Her actions have seen her become one of the greatest women footballers of all-time.

WHAT IMPACT HAS SAM KERR HAD ON THE GAME?

John: Sam has been able to influence immense structural change for women. Her genius on the pitch and her magnetism off it help embed principles such as gender equality – because who can argue she's not financially the equivalent of any male player. She has inspired a generation of girls, and boys, to believe that an Aussie can be the best footballer in the world. It has shown these same boys that the young girls in their lives deserve to be on the football pitch alongside them. As we know, finding space in football hasn't always been easy for girls and women. Through Sam, they are finding their space and finding their voice to shape their sport.

'Sam is mainly known for her speed, tenacity and skill. She is a "complete forward", which means she sees and takes opportunities to push possession forward. Sam does this by going deep to bring her teammates into play or by running the channels, as she is an excellent reader of the match. This makes her the team's focal point, as she can create space for them.'

FORMER TEAMMATE

WOMEN IN FOOTBALL

- The number of women and girls playing football has risen to record numbers, with participation in Australia climbing to more than 1.95 million in 2019.
- Football has been played in Australia since the 1800s, with more than 2 million people currently playing football in our country. For children aged six to thirteen, football has a participation rate of 48.7%, making it just as popular as swimming for the most-played sport in that age group.
- The best age for a girl to start playing in a football team is between the ages of six and nine years old. Studies show there is an advantage to children starting in that age bracket as they have by that time developed a solid attention span, have stronger vision and coordination, and have hopefully mastered sharing.
- As of June 2021, football was the most popular women's sport globally.
- Football is a healthy and empowering activity for girls.
- There are now more than 2200 football clubs in Australia.
- Women make up 22% of Australia's football participation base.
- After years of underfunding, female football is expected to have a huge surge of interest off the back of the 2023 FIFA Women's World Cup.
- More than 26,350 women and girls are currently signed up to play football in Australia, with that number increasing rapidly.

'I just want to prove to people that women's sport is right up there.'

SAM KERR

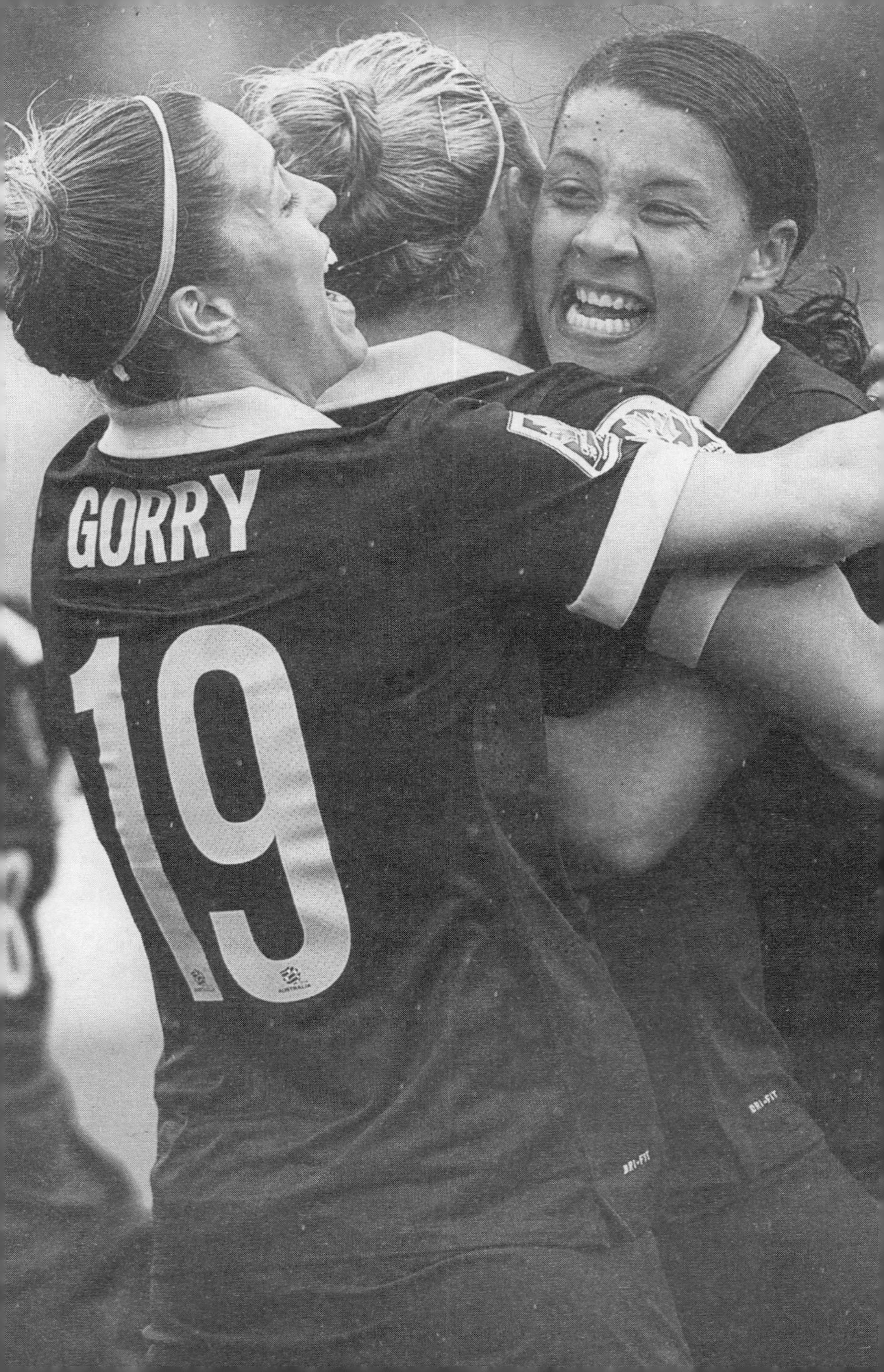
GORRY
19

CLUBS, TEAMS AND COMPS

In the lead-up to the 2023 World Cup, I've been thinking a lot about all the teams and big competitions I've been lucky enough to play with, and in, over the years. From Perth Glory to Chelsea, from Sky Blue FC to the Matildas, and in amazing tournaments like the Asian Cup and the Olympics, my football journey has been exciting, varied and challenging.

I was eighteen the first time I left Australia to play in the inaugural season of the US NWSL (National Women's Soccer League) with the Western New York Flash team. It was an amazing opportunity for a young girl like me to be able to go overseas and play alongside American soccer superstars (and now dear friends) like Carli Lloyd and Abby Wambach. We ended up winning the NWSL Shield. Other American clubs I played for in the years that followed were the Sky Blue Football Club in New Jersey and the Chicago Red Stars. The time I spent playing soccer in the USA was a huge learning curve for me, and I'm so grateful for the experiences and opportunities I had there.

When I was asked to join the New York Flash, I remember how sad I felt to have to be so far away from my family. Leaving my home to go to the other side of the world at such a young age was a big adjustment because I'm so close to my family and missed them all very much. But I also knew that if I wanted to commit myself to this sport, then being away from my loved ones was a sacrifice I was going to have to make, especially if I was going to play at the level I wanted to.

When I was playing in America, I'd spend the northern summer in New Jersey, and then fly back to Perth in October to play for my home team. At any time during the year, I could be playing international matches anywhere in the world, including China, Germany, Cyprus or Brazil, and even though I'm one of those people who hates flying, there's no way I'd ever complain about all the amazing opportunities I've had, and the different countries I've been able to visit. I'm also grateful for all the fantastic experiences I've had with my various coaches, teammates and teams over the years. Every single one of those people have played an important part in my career and have contributed towards making me the player I am today.

I guess the most significant team and club for me as a player came during my time with Sky Blue in 2017. That season, I could feel myself really growing as a player. I ended up scoring seventeen goals, which earned me the Golden Boot and Most Valued Player awards. That year, I also notched up four goals in one half in a game against Seattle, which we won 5–4. The reason that year sticks in my mind and was so significant for me is because that was the year I was moved to the number 9 position (striker) on the pitch. Before that, I was always on the wing, but as soon as I moved, it felt like I'd found my position. It just felt so right, and I knew that this was where I should be. It made all the difference to my game and my confidence.

But I also felt a lot of pressure that year. I had a reputation by then for scoring goals, and so whenever I was playing a game there was always this fear and a paranoia that I wouldn't be able to do that. Before the Tournament of Nations in 2017, I'd always played really well for Perth Glory but not really well for the national team. I started worrying that my teammates thought I was no good when I didn't score for them, so I started talking to a sport psychologist. The Matildas coach, Alen Stajcic, brought her on so that any of us could talk to her whenever we were having these doubts and fears and insecurities, and she was just amazing. She told me not to visualise scoring goals, because it can be so disappointing when I don't actually. Instead, she told me just to go out there and enjoy playing the game. It worked. Instead of spending all my time in the change room before a game, stressing and feeling anxious, I would just take a ball in there with me and play cricket or handball instead of getting mentally hung up on the game I was about to play.

When we were about to go out and play Japan in that tournament, Caitlin asked me if I was going to score that day. I looked at her and said, 'I'm going to score three.' I ended up playing my best game ever for the national team that day, and I know it was because of what the psychologist told me and how she helped me. I have a chat with her now before every game I play and it always helps. Over the years, I've made so many special and long-lasting friendships and connections, just like the one I have with my psycologist. Whether it's the teammates I've played with, the coaches who've trained me, or people who work at the clubs I've been a part of, I've been so lucky.

'She's an inspirational leader. As an Australian football community, we should be thankful we're witnessing one of the best players in the world live. She got her rewards and fully deserved it. She's a special one. It's history. All of the accolades must go to her but also the service she got from the rest of the team.'

Ante Milicic, coach of the Australian
national women's football team, 2019–2020

SAM'S SENIOR CAREER CLUBS AND STATS

1. Matildas U17	12 appearances	4 goals
2. Matildas U20	12 appearances	4 goals
3. Sydney FC	24 appearances	13 goals
4. Western New York Flash	41 appearances	15 goals
5. Sky Blue FC	40 appearances	28 goals
6. Perth Glory	71 appearances	57 goals
7. Chicago Red Stars	43 appearances	35 goals
8. Matildas	118 appearances	62 goals
9. Chelsea	107 appearances	85 goals
CAREER TOTAL	462 appearances	300 goals

CHELSEA

Towards the end of 2019, I signed with Chelsea Football Club of England's top-division, the FA Women's Super League (WSL). It was a big life choice to make and one that actually took me two years to make. Chelsea's manager, Emma Hayes, courted me and wanted me to join much earlier than I actually did, but I wasn't ready. Emma didn't give up though and we communicated back and forth for over a year.

I love Emma. We have a great, open and honest relationship and she always gets the best out of me. When we were communicating over the phone during the time before I came to Chelsea, we were very serious because we were both trying to impress each other, but now we know each other so well, it's more relaxed and chilled between us.

More than anything, I love the honesty that exists between us. Neither of us are the kind of people who like to beat around the bush. We both tell it like it is and speak our minds, which is why there is so much mutual respect between us.

Starting with Chelsea was great, but it was also challenging. Not only because of Covid, but because I had a leg injury – a quadriceps strain – and also because I wasn't used to the freezing cold conditions in England. Playing with Chelsea was a big change from my other teams, and more mentally challenging than anything. I was trying to adjust to not only my new team, but also a new country, culture and house.

I was way out of my comfort zone, and it didn't help that I didn't know a single person when I first arrived. It was quite lonely and full on to be going through all of that without my family or friends around me. I thought playing football in England would be similar to playing at home or in the USA, but it was extremely different. Football is a much more physical game in England and the tackles are fierce. That first month at Chelsea was really hard but it didn't take long before I knew that I'd made the right choice to leave Australia and come to England. Joining Chelsea is a decision I've never regretted. It's the best club I've ever been part of and I can't imagine playing for any other club in the league now.

Once I got my leg injury under control and was more used to this new, more aggressive style of playing, I felt much better. I scored twenty-one goals in twenty-two games that season, and we won our fifth title in May 2021. We also appeared in the Champions League final that year but unfortunately lost to Barcelona in the title match.

I was so honoured to receive the Golden Boot award as the WSL's top scorer that year, especially because I had copped a bit of flak from the critics, who had doubted that I would be able to cut it in the Women's Super League. I'd like to think that my performance on the pitch that year put their doubts to rest!

Since I've started playing with Chelsea, we've won eight trophies with the club, including back-to-back-to-back Women's Super League titles, and reaching the UEFA Women's Champions League final for the first time ever in 2021. I love playing with Chelsea and hope I can continue playing with them for a long time to come.

'Emma's an amazing coach but also an amazing person – someone who takes care of us on and off the pitch. She cares a lot about us as people, which I think allows us to perform to our best. She's tough though, and definitely gets after you if you're not doing what you should be doing! Part of the reason for joining Chelsea was that I knew Emma would challenge me, the club would challenge me and the league would challenge me. It's only bettered my game. I've had to adapt and I've definitely got stronger for it.'

Sam Kerr

A SUPER ROLE MODEL: AN INTERVIEW WITH CHELSEA FC MANAGER AND COACH, EMMA HAYES

TELL US ABOUT WHEN YOU FIRST MET SAM?

Emma: The first time I met Sam in person was when she came to sign her contract with Chelsea Football Club at the end of 2019, but we had actually been communicating over text messages for a year before that. I was trying to convince her to join the team, so I told her that it doesn't rain as much in London as people think it does. I knew that was one of her biggest worries, coming from a sunny place like Australia. I told her that as an Australian she would love London because there are so many Australians here. I told her about my life growing up in London and working in Covent Garden for most of my life, and how there is a humungous Aussie community here and that she'd feel very settled. I think there are people who have a misconception about rain in our country but actually it's just grey a lot. What I didn't tell Sam was that there are less sunny days!

She loves London now – I think having her fellow Matildas here up the road helps and I think she's embraced London for what it is. As I had expected, when we finally met in person, Sam and I instantly clicked.

WHY DO YOU THINK THAT WAS?

Emma: I think that Sam and I have the same kind of work ethic and we also share the same values. It was an instant connection between us, and one where I understood immediately how ambitious Sam was, and how much she wanted to win. But I also knew that wanting the best for the team was at the heart of everything Sam ever did and said, as well as wanting to belong and fit in. That was probably more important to her at the time than the winning. That really resonated with me because, for someone as high profile as Sam Kerr, she certainly valued and respected the things that I believe are the most important.

HAVE YOU MET SAM'S PARENTS?

Emma: I met Sam's parents when we won the FA Cup, and as I was listening to a conversation that Sam's dad was having with my dad, I remember thinking, 'Oh, now I know where she comes from, I can totally understand her and relate to her in so many ways'. I give full and huge credit to her parents and family – they've done an amazing job raising her and I know that she gets all of her best qualities and strengths from them. Her parents are brilliant.

'She is a superb athlete, an amazing human and these are only two of her many, many characteristics. Champions don't make excuses; Sam takes responsibility, she is in control. There is no way she is going to be on the losing team. We are extremely lucky to have her at this club.'

EMMA HAYES

WHAT'S IT LIKE FOR YOU AS A COACH HAVING SAM ON THE TEAM?

Emma: Sam is an absolute joy to coach. I think she epitomises everything you'd want at a club the size of Chelsea. She carries the badge with enormous pride and represents it in the most diverse way. Sam is unique. She's a unique character and I wouldn't swap her for anyone else in the world, in so many ways. I love her dearly. I'm forty-six years old with a four-year-old child, so it's not as if I want to hang out with my players socially, no disrespect, but I'd be there for Sam whenever she needs me. If she ever needs to get things off her chest, I'm there. I have huge respect for Sam, and will always listen to her and talk through anything she wants to talk about. On the pitch she's a champion, and she trains like a champion, too. People often ask me, 'What separates the best from the rest?' I always say that it's mentality and training habits, and Sam has those in abundance. She trains like she's a first-year pro, like she's got something to prove. I figured out not to overwhelm her with details – she's a creative and expressive person – so I've got to give her the freedom to be able to be at her best, and to try to bring the best out of her with the team around her. She's a super role model – at every game she's always one of the last players to stay out there signing autographs and I mean EVERY week. Sam takes her position and her responsibility in a way that you could only ask, and I'm talking a BIG time player, but she doesn't act like it, thank goodness.

ANY FINAL WORDS ABOUT SAM?

Emma: I think Australia should treasure her and should want to keep her playing for as long as she can, because she's worth her weight in gold to your country. The way Sam represents Australia and England globally is so positive. She's worth everything and more.

THE OLYMPICS

I wasn't sure I was going to end up making it to the 2016 Olympics in Rio de Janeiro. During the first half of a Perth Glory W-League match at Suncorp Stadium against Brisbane Roar in November 2015, I was running down the pitch when I heard a pop in my left foot. Afterwards, it felt like my foot was in two pieces and was so painful. An X-ray showed that I'd suffered a Lisfranc fracture – the rupture of a tendon that supports the bones – immediately ruling me out for the rest of the season.

To say I was gutted was an understatement, especially since I'd only just recovered from a knee injury at the end of the previous season. I'd done so much work to get back on track and now here I was, injured again and possibly out of the running for the Olympics squad.

I had to go through four surgeries, including having a plate and four screws inserted into my foot. It was one of the toughest and darkest periods of my life. I knew there was no guarantee that I'd ever be able to play football again, and that was devastating to me. I had taken my career for granted. When I was lying there, unable to play, I realised that football was a huge and important part of my life, and had given me so many opportunities. I wasn't ready to say goodbye.

I'd been ruled out of the Olympics qualifying campaign in February but knew there was still a chance I could make it back to training in time for the Rio Olympic qualifiers in March. It became a race against the clock for me to recover in time for the qualifiers, as well as for the Matildas' major tournament.

I'd been dreaming of playing in the Olympics since I was a young kid. I was determined to get my foot back in top shape by then. But after my fourth and final surgery, I started noticing the difference. It was already feeling much better just a few days after surgery.

Just in the nick of time I was ready, fit and recovered enough to make the final eighteen-player Matildas squad for the 2016 Rio Olympics.

The Matildas were drawn in Group F against Canada, Germany and Zimbabwe, and lost our first game, 0–2, against Canada. We did better in our next match, drawing with Germany, 2–2 and then absolutely slayed it in our third game against Zimbabwe, winning 6–1. This result meant that we had finished third in our group, making it through to the quarterfinals.

'The thought of missing out on the opportunity to make the eighteen-player Olympic squad was devastating. I was determined to get my foot back in top shape.'

SAM KERR

We faced the tournament's host Brazil in that match and it was a tough and, ultimately, heartbreaking game. The game ended with a tense penalty shoot-out after 120 minutes of play in ordinary and extra time, and sadly we lost, 7–6. But we were so proud of ourselves because we knew we had given it everything we had. I was so honoured to play alongside those amazing footballers and wouldn't have missed out on playing, despite the loss, for anything.

The 2020 Olympics were obviously the most memorable for everyone around the world, mainly because, for the first time in history, they couldn't take place due to a global pandemic. Instead, the 2020 Olympics in Tokyo took place in 2021. The Matildas were grouped with the USA, Sweden and New Zealand, and in our first game we beat New Zealand, 2–1. In our second game against Sweden, I was gutted to miss a penalty. We ended up losing that game, 4–2, but still progressed into the quarter-finals against Great Britain.

It was an intense game and at the eighty-ninth minute I scored an equaliser goal, putting the game into extra time. Shortly after that, I was lucky enough to score another goal, securing our team's 4–3 victory. Our semifinal match against Sweden broke women's sport TV viewing records in Australia, with more than 2 million people tuning in to watch. During that game, I scored a goal that was controversially disallowed. We ended up losing that game, 1–0.

In the bronze medal match, we lost 4–3 to the USA, and ended up finishing fourth overall. Despite this, we were incredibly proud of our efforts as a team, especially knowing that Olympic history had been made, with records broken both on and off the pitch. Our fourth-place finish was the Matildas' best result ever at an Olympic Games.

THIS KID HAS GOT SOMETHING: AN INTERVIEW WITH SAM'S PERTH GLORY COACH, BOBBY DESPOTOVSKI

TELL US ABOUT THE FIRST TIME YOU SAW SAM ON A FOOTBALL PITCH?

Bobby: I knew Sam from before I started coaching her, not personally but I would watch her when she was playing for Perth Glory when she was just fourteen years old. The under 15s Perth Glory team trained on the ground near where I lived and I'd often go for walks around that ground with my wife and kids. I would see Sam and watch training sessions, and she was extraordinary to watch. From the beginning, she stood out. At that stage, I was still active and playing for Perth Glory and I remember thinking, *This kid has got something*. She was extraordinarily fast – much faster than anybody else – and obviously that catches your eye straight away. It's hard not to notice when somebody is that explosive and fast, and it was pleasing to see.

WHEN DID YOU START COACHING SAM?

Bobby: When I finished my career playing for Perth Glory, I went into coaching some of the junior and senior sides at the club, until I eventually became the coach for the Perth Glory Women's team, and she was in that side.

WHAT KIND OF PLAYER WAS SAM LIKE TO COACH?

Bobby: As a player, she was amazing to coach, purely because she wanted to progress and learn and go to the next level. Obviously, the next level at that time was America, and she was already playing with Chicago and wanted to improve. The first big change in Sam, and improvement, happened in that first year I was coaching her. That's when she began to sort out her 'off the field' stuff that she needed to address, and at the time she was twenty one years old. She had made a decision then that she wanted to concentrate on football 100% of the time.

WHAT DID YOU DO DIFFERENTLY?

Bobby: The first thing we did was change her position from winger to striker. Sam started her career in football as a winger due to her incredible speed but I converted her to a striker. Since I was a striker in my heyday, I could give her pointers on where and how she could improve – and she took that all in her stride.

'Sammy's got everything. Her athleticism and raw talent is exceptional and she is tremendously fast.'

BOBBY DESPOTOVSKI

She just wanted to get better, and her commitment and discipline were sensational. There is no motivation for Sam Kerr that you need to address – she knows what she needs to do. She knows she wants to reach the pinnacle – to be the best footballer in the world – and she just works very, very hard.

We had a very good professional relationship – whatever my experience gave me I wanted to pass that on to her – and if she took that and improved on it, that was great. I just wanted to provide the opportunity and information to her. What she did with it was up to her.

I was a big believer in her and knew she could be the best footballer in the world – and now that she is close to it, I think she might believe it more than she did when I told her that when I was coaching her.

WILL YOU BE WATCHING THE WORLD CUP IN 2023?

Bobby: Yes, I'll be watching the groups here in Perth and if they progress into the finals, I'll definitely go to see the World Cup games. Even now, whenever Sam does a great thing with Chelsea FC, I send her a text message congratulating her or I reach out to her on Facebook.

'Sam's speed change is astronomical; I haven't seen anything like it, especially in a female footballer.'

BOBBY DESPOTOVSKI

THE BACKFLIP QUEEN

Anyone who knows me will tell you that I'm actually a pretty reserved and quiet person, but as soon as I get out on the pitch it's like my extroverted and crazy side comes out. I shout, dance, run around in circles, take off my top and fling it around, knee slide, or – the one I've become most known for – backflip.

I've been able to do backflips for as long as I can remember. Back from when I just a small kid, I have memories of practising doing backflips over and over in my backyard at home, or on the oval at primary school, stressing out both my parents and teachers in the process.

Most of the time, my reaction to a goal is completely spontaneous and backflipping in particular is instinctive – my automatic response to the adrenaline, and the joy and excitement rushing through my whole body. Sometimes I don't even know I'm going to do it until I find myself flying upside down through the air.

I remember the first time I ever did a backflip after a goal during a game of football. It felt so natural. And I've been doing them ever since.

The first time the world got to see my now-famous post-goal backflip was when I scored my first goal for the Matildas at the 2010 AFC Asian Cup in a game against South Korea. I was so excited, it just happened!

In 2022 when I scored a hat-trick for Chelsea I celebrated with my trademark backflip but it hadn't been on my mind at the time. At half-time, one of my team members said, 'If you score the hat-trick, can you please do it?' I hadn't done a backflip for such a long time but it was a night worth celebrating. I will remember it forever.

SAM'S VITAL STATS

Full name: Samantha May Kerr

Birth: 10 September 1993

Hometown: Fremantle

Schools attended: Samson Primary School and Kennedy Baptist College (previously Somerville Baptist College)

Family members:

  Parents: Roger, Roxanne

  Siblings: Daniel, Levi, Madeline

AFL team: West Coast Eagles

Hobbies: Spending time with family and friends, playing with my dog, drinking coffee and taste-testing nice food

Sporting influences: Cathy Freeman (because she's a legend), Cristiano Ronaldo (because his ability to be consistent year after year is so impressive) and Serena Williams (because she's always on her A-game. She's a supreme athlete and just a hungry person).

Hollywood crush: Gerard Butler

Downtime faves: Coffee, friends, shopping, Netflix

THE MATILDAS
AND TEAMWORK

When you're playing a team sport, any team sport, not just football, teamwork is the most important thing. Working together, rather than as individuals, is what it's all about, and the support you get from your teammates, as well as the support you give them, is the most rewarding and enjoyable part of any team sport. Knowing that my teammates are always there, watching my back and supporting me on and off the pitch, is the best feeling ever.

If you're part of a fantastic team, like I am so lucky to be, the people you play with become so much more than just teammates. They become your best friends. So many of the amazing experiences I've had over the years with my friends and teammates are the ones I'll remember for the rest of my life, long after I've retired from playing football. I've learned so much from the people I've played with out on the pitch, but I've also had a great time with them off the field as well. My teammates and I love to make our training sessions fun. There are lots of jokes and laughter while we're out there working hard, and when we're competing against other teams, too.

The best thing about being part of a team is that you get to share your good times and the not-so-good times with each other, rather than dealing with it alone. I often think about how hard it must be sometimes to play a solo sport, such as tennis or boxing, when it's just you out there front and centre. When things aren't going so great and you're losing matches, there's no one to share the losses with and it's just you alone who has to deal with how that feels. When you are part of a team, there is a very strong team spirit among everyone, which means that you can share all your achievements, and your failures, with each other. You celebrate the wins and commiserate the losses, and the more difficult times, together.

Since I've become captain of the Matildas, my main focus has been on keeping that team spirit alive and making sure that the bond we've all created with each other stays as solid as ever. Although this kind of leadership role means that I have more responsibility, and that I have to be more demanding of my team at times, I still try to be a good role model for my teammates and make them feel like they can talk to me about anything that's worrying them. Sometimes it's a hard balance to achieve, but I always try my best.

'I can't explain how proud I am to be a part of this team and to lead this team out.'

SAM KERR, CAPTAIN OF THE MATILDAS

MATILDAS CAMP REGIME

Before the Matildas head off to play big tournaments overseas, we lock down for 'camp'. This camp consists of intensive training, team meetings and other events, all done together as a squad. At the camp, the players dart back and forth between training sessions, meals and meetings, and the support staff are just as busy as the players.

CAMP GOALS

- Train twice a day.
- High-intensity sessions focusing on gameplay and team structures.
- Light afternoon session where players break off to focus on technical details.
- Strikers focus on shooting.
- Defenders focus on defence work.
- Prepare for upcoming games.
- Review matches and training sessions.
- Team-bonding sessions.
- Working on base strength is a vital part of the game.
- Eating healthy.

'There are no hierarchies, there are no cliques, it is everyone together. We are fit and we are fast. That's where women's football is going at the moment. It is fast and aggressive.'

SAM KERR

MY TEAMMATE SAM: AN INTERVIEW WITH CAITLIN FOORD

TELL US ABOUT WHEN YOU FIRST MET SAM?

Caitlin: I first met Sam in Canberra at the U17 Australian Youth Camp. She stood out because she used to wear a full-colour beanie that had sides on it (I think they call it a trapper hat) or if she wasn't wearing that, she had a cap that always faced backwards.

WHAT IS SAM LIKE AS A TEAMMATE?

Caitlin: Sam is the teammate everyone would love to have. She doesn't take things too seriously, and she makes everyone feel included and valued. Sam is the joker of the team and brings a lot of energy to the team.

WHAT ARE SAM'S STRENGTHS AS A CAPTAIN?

Caitlin: Sam's strengths as a captain are making everyone feel included and valued. But her main strength is that she leads by her actions.

WHAT IS SAM LIKE AS A FRIEND, AWAY FROM THE GAME?

Caitlin: Away from the game, Sam is an easy-going, always up for anything type of person. She loves a good time and is super reliable. I know if I had to call her about anything, she would be there for me

TELL US ABOUT YOUR MOST MEMORABLE MOMENT WITH SAM AT A GAME?

Caitlin: There are so many, it's hard to pick one. But I think on the pitch when we link up, create and score goals. We have played together for so many years now that it just comes naturally.

WHAT DO YOU NEED TO DO TO WIN?

Caitlin: Keep calm, be patient, be confident and the goals will come.

WHAT IS THE BEST ADVICE SAM HAS GIVEN YOU?

Caitlin: I wouldn't say it's advice but when I wasn't in a great phase in my career and was feeling very low in confidence, she made me believe how good I am and helped me gain my confidence back.

WHAT ARE YOU ALL, AS A TEAM, MOST EXCITED ABOUT IN THE LEAD-UP TO THE WORLD CUP?

Caitlin: I think we are all super excited to be working together again. We usually play against each other for different teams, but to come together for this once-in-a-lifetime opportunity is so exciting!

WHAT IS THE BEST THING ABOUT PLAYING IN FRONT OF A HOME CROWD AS A TEAM?

Caitlin: I think the best part is knowing that our family and friends are amongst the crowd. We play overseas so often that it's rare they get to watch us live. So this is always a special moment for us and our families.

WHAT DO YOU THINK IS SAM'S BIGGEST STRENGTH AS A PLAYER?

Caitlin: Sam's biggest strength is that she is so unpredictable. It makes it difficult for defenders to know what she's doing. Also her ability in front of goal is world class. She can finish in every way. So as her teammate you just know to get her the ball. If it's in the air or along the ground it doesn't matter. And she's a winner.

YOU AND SAM HAVE PLAYED TOGETHER ALL AROUND THE WORLD. WHAT IS YOUR MOST MEMORABLE MOMENT TOGETHER DURING YOUR TRAVELS?

Caitlin: I think the 2011 World Cup. We were both really young and it was our first World Cup. Just to experience that together was very special. And now, many years on, we have been to three World Cups and two Olympic Games together. It is pretty special to share all these big occasions and experiences with Sam.

2022 ASIAN CUP

In January 2022, the Matildas had a devastating shock loss when we crashed out of the AFC Women's Asian Cup when we lost our quarterfinal match against South Korea 1–0. It was our worst-ever result in the competition and a very hard pill to swallow. We were all heartbroken, especially since we'd dominated in the first half of the match. But it just wasn't meant to be. Even when we were playing well in the first half, we just couldn't get a goal in. We hit the cross bar and got a few calls against us. In the second half of the match, we didn't play as well as the first half. At some point we all had a sense that nothing we did was working for us and we just couldn't get a goal in. I know that's just part of playing sport, and not every match goes the way you want it to, but it still sucks.

I found that loss hard to shake off, even after I arrived back at Chelsea. Suddenly I was back in England, playing in games with my team that I had assumed I'd be watching on TV from India. I felt so upset that I couldn't watch any of the Asian Cup games after that.

But that's football, and any sport really. You just can't always score every goal you go for, and you're always going to have times when you fail. It's a sad fact of life and the only thing you can do is get back up and try again. There's no other choice. Even after that disappointing loss, I still had faith in us as a team. You just have to keep going, and not dwell on the losses and the missed opportunities. It doesn't do you, or your game, any good.

We know we should have performed better at the Asian Cup in 2022 but we still felt like we gave it everything up until the last fifteen minutes of the game. It was incredibly disappointing, but we're committed to sticking together, and believe in ourselves as a team.

'I always believe in this team. I give everything for the national team and I know every single player does – like we wouldn't be playing overseas and missing our families for two years if we didn't want to win for the national team. I'd be home on the first flight if I didn't have the national team. I wouldn't be doing all of this just for fun!'

Sam Kerr

SAM'S TOP TIPS FOR MANAGING DISAPPOINTMENT

1. Think positive thoughts.
2. Get back out and train and play.
3. Set boundaries.
4. Take time to recharge.
5. Prioritise your time.
6. Take time away from social media.
7. Spend time with family and friends.

MIND OVER MATTER

When it comes to my profession as an athlete, there's one thing, one key ingredient, that motivates me more than anything else. The one thing that drives me to get up and out of bed in the morning, no matter how terrible the weather is, and go to training. There's one thing that drives me to eat well, look after my body, and stay fit and healthy, which drives me to keep going even when things might not be going as well as I want them to. That one thing is winning.

There have been lots of times throughout my career when I've felt down, stressed or under a lot of pressure, just like everyone does at some point in their lives. There have been lots of times when I'm upset because our team hasn't won, or when I'm feeling nervous and have zero confidence before a game. It's times like these when I try and use mind over matter to stay motivated and driven. I try to shift my focus to the task at hand – that one match or that one training session or that one goal – and stay focused on it. Staying in the present and focusing on that one thing isn't easy but it definitely helps. I just have to believe in what I'm doing, and try to ignore any distracting, negative or outside factors that start to creep in. Using this mental tool to maintain this kind of attitude is a big factor in winning for me. I truly believe that.

Above all else, I need to try and stay focused on what I can control, rather than worrying about the things that I can't, especially when I'm under a lot of pressure during a tournament. For example, when we were playing against Jamaica in the 2019 World Cup, we chose not to find out the outcome of the Brazil game until the end of our match. That let us focus on the task at hand and not concern ourselves with something that we had no control over. I knew then that if I'd found out the result of the Brazil game, it would have gotten in my head and possibly distracted me from what I was doing, so I didn't.

I understand now just how important it is to try and have a positive attitude, both on and off the field. Firstly, it makes it much easier to deal with stress and negative situations in a healthy way. I'm better able to deal with disappointments and failures by accepting how things turn out and moving on, rather than dwelling on them and getting stuck and bogged down in that negative result. For example, I hate missing goals and always feel hugely disappointed when I do, but I also know that there's no point staying focused on that missed goal after it happens. As soon as the ball doesn't hit the back of the net, I have to motivate myself to keep going and put all my focus on the next task at hand. Most of the time, I succeed in doing this and manage to bounce back, thank goodness. If I was to list my main strengths as an athlete, I would say they are my drive, my athleticism and my attitude, but that doesn't mean it's always easy to maintain those strengths, especially in today's world. There's so much pressure involved in the business of being an athlete these days when it comes to social media and the 24/7 news cycle.

Unfortunately, many top athletes end up being targets of a lot of online hate and criticism, which can be incredibly draining and upsetting for the individual and their families and friends. As a professional athlete at the top of your game, if you looked at and read everything said about you online, it would have a damaging and toxic impact on your mental state, and that would have an impact on your game. Someone might be an amazing athlete and a global superstar, but they are still a human being.

I'm fully aware of my own weaknesses as an athlete. I know that I tend to play well if I walk out onto that pitch in a happy frame of mind. But I can be too competitive a lot of the time, which can be a negative thing, especially when I put too much pressure on myself.

I know there were a lot of people who got really upset and angry when I didn't make the three-player final shortlist for

FIFA's Best Women's Player in 2017, but I tried not to let it get to me. At the end of the day, someone is always going to be upset when those kinds of awards are given out, and I know that kind of stuff isn't really important anyway, not as important as something like winning the World Cup. I think it's really crucial not to let that kind of stuff get inside your head because it messes with you. When you play sport on a professional level and you're all over the news and on TV, it's very easy to get caught up in it all and get a big head, but I don't want to be that person. I need to stay true to who I am.

I know how important it is for me to keep working hard on myself, and not just on my physical fitness but on my mental health, too. I want to set myself up for the future. I also want to be happy. I know that this is more important than winning games, fame, or awards and accolades. I love what I do but I also know that it's not healthy to always be thinking about football. That wouldn't be a realistic or satisfying kind of life. When I'm home I need to be able to switch off, which is why I try not to talk about the game or anything to do with football when I'm with my family and friends.

'It's important
to take time away
from football to
refresh when you're
a professional
athlete. Don't let
it consume you.'

SAM KERR

SAM'S TOP TIPS FOR MANAGING STRESS AND PRESSURE

- Get a good night's sleep.
- Take regular breaks from your phone.
- Focus on things you can control.
- Stay off social media.
- Have a good routine that makes you feel prepared.

'Don't worry about things you can't control.'

SAM KERR

Sam's dog Billie, a boxer, still lives at home in Perth.

Sam getting up close and personal with a quokka on Rottnest Island, Western Australia.

Sam playing at the Qantas National Youth Championships for Girls.

Learning how to juggle a football is the first step to becoming a striker like Sam.

Sam always tries to go home to Perth in the off season for some relaxing holidays.

Relaxing on Rottnest Island.

Sam's mum Roxanne has always been one of her biggest supporters.

Sam Kerr's nanna, Coral, migrated from India with her husband and children.

Sam is a proud auntie and loves catching up with her nieces and nephews.

Family time is
precious when you
live so far away.

Sam loves travelling with her partner, Kristie Mews.

Kristie is also a football star, who has played for the US Women's National Team.

Winning the ESPY (Excellence in Sports Performance Yearly) in 2018. She also won it in 2019 and 2022.

MEMORABLE MOMENTS

There have been so many amazing and memorable football playing moments over the years for me, it would be impossible to list all of them, but a few definitely stand out in my mind.

PLAYING IN THE OFC WOMEN'S CHAMPIONSHIP TOURNAMENT

In 1998, I played for Australia in the Oceania Football Confederation (OFC) Women's Championship tournament. We ended up winning the final match, 3–1, against New Zealand, qualifying for the 1999 FIFA Women's World Cup in the USA for the first time. I'll never forget how exciting that feeling was.

MY W-LEAGUE DEBUT WITH PERTH GLORY

Three years after I swapped from playing AFL, I made my W-League debut for Perth Glory on 25 October 2008 at 15 years of age. To this day, I hold the Australian record for being the youngest player on a W-League team.

MY FIRST MATILDAS GOAL IN 2010

My first goal for the Matildas happened at the 2010 Asian Football Confederation (AFC) Asian Cup in a game against South Korea. It was also the first time the world got to see my now-famous post-goal backflip!

WINNING THE WOMEN'S ASIAN CUP IN 2010

The Matildas won the AFC Women's Asian Cup against Korea in 2010, which was Australia's first win for either men or women's football since joining the AFC in 2005.

WINNING THE PFA WOMEN'S FOOTBALLER OF THE YEAR AWARD IN 2013

The Professional Footballers Australia (PFA) Women's Footballer of the Year is an annual award that is given out to the person who is judged as being the best player that year in Australian football. I won it in 2013 and went on to win it another four times over the years. I'm the only player to win it in consecutive seasons and to win it that many times.

PLAYING IN WORLD CUPS AND AT THE OLYMPICS

The Matildas have represented Australia seven times in the FIFA Women's World Cup and four times at the Olympic Games. Although we haven't won at these tournaments, they are experiences I'll never forget for as long as I live.

'Never say die.'

THE MATILDAS TEAM QUOTE

WINNING YOUNG AUSTRALIAN OF THE YEAR

In 2018, I was named the Young Australian of the Year for my role as a leader and advocate for women's sports. This prestigious award recognises exceptional young Australians who are an inspiration to others. I was the first female footballer to win this award. Accepting the award in Canberra on Australia Day, I felt very proud and humbled by the honour.

BREAKING THE AUSTRALIAN ALL-TIME GOAL SCORER RECORD

One of my proudest achievements was becoming the top international goal scorer for Australia (male or female), when I overtook Tim Cahill's record of 50 international goals in our Asian Cup match against Indonesia on 21 January 2022. Our 18–0 win took my tally to 54 goals, after I scored five goals in the match with a hat-trick in the first half. I celebrated this record-breaking achievement by shadow-boxing the corner flag in honour of Cahill's famous goal celebrations.

BACK-TO-BACK GOLDEN BOOTS IN THE USA AND ENGLAND

From 2017 to 2022, I made history by winning back-to-back Golden Boot awards on two different continents, scoring the most goals in a season in both the USA and England. I won my first Golden Boot in the National Women's Soccer League in 2017, scoring 17 goals for Sky Blue FC. I repeated the feat in 2018, scoring 16 goals for Chicago Red Stars. In 2019, despite missing some club matches to play for Australia, I topped the league for the third consecutive year with 18 goals. After moving to Chelsea at the end of 2019, I won my first Golden Boot in the Women's Super League in 2020–21, scoring 21 goals in 22 games. I backed this up in 2021–22, with a result of 20 goals in 20 matches.

SCORING 50 GOALS IN THE WOMEN'S SUPER LEAGUE IN APRIL 2023

When Chelsea won 3–0 at Aston Villa, I became only the ninth woman and the first from outside Europe to score 50 goals in the English Women's Super League.

HOSTING THE WORLD CUP IN 2023

I am so proud that Australia has been chosen to co-host the 2023 FIFA Women's World Cup along with New Zealand. For the first time, there will be 32 teams playing and it is shaping up to be our biggest moment as a team yet.

AN INTERVIEW WITH SAM KERR

IF YOU COULD CHOOSE ANY TEAM PLAYING IN THE WORLD CUP, WHO WOULD YOU LIKE TO FACE IN THE FINAL (AND WIN)?

Sam: The USA! I would love to face the world champions!

HOW DIFFERENT IS IT PLAYING IN A BIG GAME FOR CHELSEA THAN PLAYING IN A WORLD CUP FOR AUSTRALIA?

Sam: It is very different but also very similar. A big game is a big game. And I love playing in big games! But playing for your country is extra special. Playing for Chelsea in big games is the closest I can get to replicating what it feels like to represent my country.

ARE YOU FEELING ANY MORE PRESSURE LEADING INTO THIS WORLD CUP THAN PREVIOUS ONES, GIVEN WE ARE CO-HOSTS AND THE HIGH EXPECTATIONS AROUND BEING ONE OF THE HOME TEAMS?

Sam: Absolutely. There is added pressure because it's a home World Cup, but it's something the team and I are welcoming. We always have such great support at home and hopefully we can use it to our advantage.

TELL US HOW IT FEELS TO PLAY IN FRONT OF A HOME CROWD?

Sam: Playing in front of friends and family is amazing. Playing in front of home fans that have watched you grow as a player is even better. It feels special being at home and playing in front of so many important people, and making so many young girls and boys so happy.

WHAT ADVICE WOULD YOU GIVE TO THE YOUNGER PLAYERS IN YOUR TEAM, WHO ARE PLAYING IN A WORLD CUP FOR THE FIRST TIME?

Sam: I would probably say, 'Just enjoy the moment and don't put too much pressure on yourself.' Staying in the moment and enjoying all the little things is so important because, before you know it, you'll be like me at your fourth World Cup!

WILL IT BE YOUR FAMOUS FLIP, KNEE SLIDE OR SOMETHING NEW WHEN YOU SCORE A GOAL?

Sam: I would like to do the backflip at a home game in the World Cup because it would be so special. But you will have to wait and see.

WHAT IS YOUR MOST MEMORABLE GOAL FROM YOUR CAREER SO FAR AND WHY?

Sam: Probably the chest volley against Man United. Just because of what was on the line, the importance of the goal and the coverage it got. It was all very exciting.

DO YOU LISTEN TO MUSIC BEFORE A GAME TO HELP YOUR MINDSET? IF SO, WHAT DO YOU LISTEN TO?

Sam: Yes, I love listening to music. I change it all the time, depending on what my favourite genre or song is at the moment. Currently, I'm listening to Burna Boy.

DO YOU GET NERVOUS BEFORE GAMES? IF SO, HOW DO YOU HANDLE NERVES?

Sam: I sometimes get nervous but nerves are good. It shows that you care. But too many nerves can become a problem. I always like to keep my mind busy and not think or play the game in my head too much beforehand. Being calm and keeping yourself focused on what you can control is very important.

WHAT WILL YOU USUALLY EAT FOR BREAKFAST ON THE MORNING OF AN IMPORTANT MATCH?

Sam: Toast, some sort of eggs, avocado and of course coffee!

CAN YOU NAME THREE INTERNATIONAL WORLD CUP PLAYERS WHO YOU ADMIRE AND WHY?

Sam: Firstly, Abby Wambach. She is an American retired big-game soccer player who I really admire. Secondly, Yuki Nagasako. She is a Japanese football player and unbelievably gifted. And of course, Caitlin Foord. We grew up playing together and she always performs at World Cups.

DO YOU WATCH *TED LASSO*? IF SO, DO YOU HAVE A FAVOURITE TED MOTTO?

Sam: I haven't watched it yet, but I do need to watch it. I live in Richmond where it was filmed.

APART FROM CATCHING UP WITH FAMILY AND FRIENDS, IS THERE SOMETHING YOU HOPE TO DO WHILE HOME FOR THE WORLD CUP?

Sam: There won't be much time for anything else. Maybe have good coffee in the different cities we visit.

WHAT IS THE BEST FEEDBACK YOU'VE HAD ABOUT YOUR NEW CHILDREN'S BOOK SERIES, KICKING GOALS?

Sam: I've really enjoyed all the young girls and boys getting to know my childhood. I love how they've realised I grew up just like them and in fact we have a lot of similarities.

'I wouldn't say
it's been smooth
sailing. It's been up
and down but it's
been enjoyable.'

SAM KERR

SAM'S TOP TIPS FOR KIDS WHO WANT TO DO WELL IN SPORT

I love inspiring kids to get into playing sport and then to play well. I had a number of role models growing up and hope I can inspire kids to follow in my footsteps. Here are my top tips to do well in sport:

WORK HARD BUT HAVE FUN

It's important to remember to have fun when you're training and playing any sport. Of course you want to be the best you can and help your team win, but you should never lose that feeling of joy and excitement that you first had when you discovered your love for that particular sport or game.

BE A GOOD TEAMMATE

When you play a team sport, it's never just about you and your own individual accomplishments. You're only as good or as strong as the team around you. Sharing the highs and lows with your teammates is a very special feeling and it's important to be the kind of team player who supports and is there for your teammates as much as you can be.

VISUALISE

Visualisation is a simple technique that you can use to create a mental image of a future event. I love to visualise myself playing well and scoring goals. I'll think about this before a game and then it happens.

NOTHING IS EVER REALLY THAT GOOD OR THAT BAD

A coach told me this once and I've never forgotten it. I take this to mean that losing a game is not the end of the world and that winning is awesome but it's not the be-all and end-all either. Having fun, being a good sportsperson and doing your best are more important than winning or losing.

'You play football to have fun, not to stress yourself out. If you work hard and have fun at the same time, you can't lose.'

SAM KERR

FAMILY AND FRIENDS

I love my family. Besides my partner, they are the most important people in my life and I miss them so much when I'm away from home, which is a lot of the time. It's even harder now that I am an aunty, too. I am lucky that I get to see my partner Kristie more than I'm able to see my family, but she has her own very successful and busy career playing football in America, so it's not always easy to catch up. I love it when she comes to watch me play. There's no greater or warmer feeling than knowing she's in the stands cheering me on.

The biggest sacrifice a professional athlete makes for their career is spending so much time every year away from loved ones. We spend so much time travelling all over the world for our games that we miss out on all those special moments and occasions at home with our families and friends.

In all the years that I've been playing professional football, I've missed out on too many birthdays, weddings, funerals, parties and births to count. That's definitely the hardest part about what I do, especially when you come from such a close family. I get homesick a lot. Mum and I have long FaceTimes every day when I'm away, and she comes over to stay with me whenever she can get the time off work. Mum and I have always been extremely close and, growing up, she was my best friend. My dad, too. He taught me everything I know about sport, and both of my parents have been pivotal in my football journey. I wouldn't be where I am today without them. They sacrificed everything for me from when I was just a young kid starting out in this sport.

And it's not only my family who I miss and don't get to celebrate special occasions with, but also my friends. It's true that I'm not your average girl. I'd rather talk sport than anything else, but I do have a bunch of great girlfriends, including my best friend, Seonaid.

Seonaid Rodgers and I met at our school, Somerville Baptist College, when we were just thirteen years old. She is still my best friend today and is now a medical physicist at Sir Charles

'The things I miss most about Australia are Tim Tams and my dog.'

Sam Kerr

Gairdner Hospital, which is so impressive and amazing. On the rare occasions when I am home, we love to just chill out together at my house with the rest of the Kerr family, eating snacks, watching TV and catching up on everything going on in our lives.

'This transformation into a really successful athlete has been weird for us [her girlfriends] because she has been the same person throughout our friendship. She comes home every summer and when we see her again, absolutely nothing has changed. She just fits right back in with us girls and doesn't tell us about her success at football, all the awards she's won and interviews she's done. Samantha is an extremely energetic, athletic person – but downtime is a big deal for her. Her family and her dog are very, very important. And she has always been that way.'

Sam's best friend, Seonaid Rodgers

Q & A WITH SAM

IF YOU WEREN'T A STRIKER, WHAT OTHER POSITION WOULD YOU PLAY ON THE FIELD AND WHY?

Sam: It would have to be goalkeeper [laughs]. Whenever there isn't a third choice in training, I go in goals. I love the fact that a goalkeeper can be the hero. The striker is either the hero or the worst player on the field, just like the goalkeeper. Goalkeepers can win or lose a game.

WHAT WAS THE FIRST PAIR OF BOOTS YOU EVER PUT ON AND WHAT EXCITES YOU MOST ABOUT THE NEW NIKE MERCURIAL DREAM SPEED BOOTS?

Sam: My first pair of boots was the Nike Total 90 and I loved them. With the new Mercurial Dream Speed, I love the bottom of the boot and I love the lightness. When it comes to boots, if they look good, I feel good and I play good. That's my motto.

YOU RUBBED SHOULDERS WITH SOME PRETTY BIG NAMES AT THE NIKE MERCURIAL LAUNCH IN LONDON. WHAT WAS IT LIKE STANDING ALONGSIDE THE LIKES OF NEYMAR AND ALEXIS SÁNCHEZ?

Sam: It was pretty surreal. I didn't get very close to Neymar but Alexis was super nice and down to earth. You sometimes forget that, off the pitch, they're just regular guys. I loved getting that selfie with the OG Ronaldo (from Brazil). I grew up watching him. He is the original and one of the best players ever. Him and Ronaldinho are what drew me to Brazilian football.

IF YOU WEREN'T PLAYING PROFESSIONAL FOOTBALL, WHAT DO YOU THINK YOU'D BE DOING?

Sam: I didn't really have a plan B. I always wanted to be a professional athlete, whether it was football or another sport. I always knew I'd end up being a professional athlete. It's all I wanted in my life. If I had to say something, I'd maybe like to be a secret agent or something really cool.

'When I first started playing football, I had a brother that was famous. So I was always known as his sister. Then all of a sudden, it changed to him being my brother.
I kind of skyrocketed in Australia, then went to America and was back down to a nobody. I went back up again and went to England as a little bit too much of a star. And then playing for a club like Chelsea, they have really elevated me.
It's been a rollercoaster, to be honest.'

SAM KERR

EA SPORTS™

FIFA 23

FIFA

OFFICIAL
LICENS
PRODU

SAM KE

HYPERMOTION2

FIFA COVER

I made history in 2022 when I was chosen to feature on the cover of FIFA 23. It was the first time a female player had ever featured on the cover. Being on the cover of a game like FIFA was a massive deal for me.

I was like 'Me? Surely not.' And then it all kind of happened so quickly that the next thing I knew, I was in Paris shooting with Kylian Mbappe!

It was so surreal, especially when it feels like my career has been such a rollercoaster ride with so many ups and downs. When I first started playing football, it was my brother who was the famous one in the Kerr family, and I was always known as Daniel's little sister. When I started becoming more well-known for football, it changed to him being Sam's brother, which was weird. But when I went to America I was a nobody again, and then slowly became more well-known. By the time I got to England

I think I was too much of a star. Playing for a club like Chelsea has elevated me. It definitely hasn't been smooth sailing, but it's been enjoyable. But the cover of FIFA is next level and more than I could ever have imagined happening for me. It really is a dream come true, especially because I've been playing this game for so long. I remember how excited I was that females were going to be included in the game, and never could have envisaged that I would be in it myself, let alone on the cover. It's such an incredible feeling and I'm so proud. This is something that I'm going to be able to look at for the rest of my life and show my kids when they are hopefully playing FIFA, too.

EA Sports have been fantastic to work with, and the fact that they are so supportive of women's football has been really important to me. So many people have reached out to me about this game, saying how cool it is to see a female on the cover, especially for all the young boys and girls growing up. It's going to just be the norm for these kids to see females represented like this in sport, which is something I never had when I was young.

Of course this kind of stuff is amazing, but it doesn't make me a good footballer or teammate. That's one thing I pride myself on, which is why I think I've always stayed down to earth, no matter what is going on with my career. I don't believe I'm better or cooler than anyone on my team or around me because I'm on the cover of FIFA. I'm just one of them and I hope that my teammates have respect for me because of how I train and play, and for the kind of person I am, not because of stuff like this. Whenever I do anything, I always am just who I am.

'As things went along, I [became] very excited . . . and the next thing I knew I was in Paris . . . and it was just a bit of a whirlwind to be honest. Only three people in my life knew. I did a seminar talking about how there needs to be a female on the cover, and I was sitting there knowing that I was lying to all of them.'

Sam Kerr

DID YOU KNOW?

On her final goal against Manchester United in May 2022, Sam swivelled in the air to volley the ball into the net.

'That's just who I am. I do that stuff like that in training all the time. Sometimes the girls get annoyed at me and sometimes it looks good, but it's just who I am. I'm a risk-taker. I just do what I feel, whether it's right or wrong, and I'm very strong willed, very stubborn. I think it's one of the best goals I've ever scored. There was no doubt in my mind that I was just hitting that ball once it came off my chest and I think that's what I mean when I say I'm a risk-taker. My whole life is lived on the edge. I either go big or go home.'

Sam Kerr

DID YOU KNOW?

Sam has only received eight yellow cards at the club football level, and only two at the national football level. She has never received a red card in all her years playing football.

'Obviously it's like a dream come true to be on the cover of FIFA. I think every kid growing up plays FIFA, whether you're a football fan or not.'

SAM KERR

WORLD CUPS

In total, eight FIFA Women's World Cups have been held since the tournament was created in 1991. Just like the Men's World Cups, they occur every four years, and national teams vie for thirty-one slots in a three-year qualification phase. The host nation's team is automatically entered as the thirty-second slot and the tournament is played out at different venues within the host nation over a period of about one month. The first Women's World Cup was hosted by China and the United States National team won that year.

Six countries have hosted the Women's World Cup so far, including China and the USA, which have each hosted the tournament twice, as well as Canada, France, Germany and Sweden. Overall, the Women's World Cup has been won by four of the national teams that participate in the tournament every time. The USA has won four times, Germany twice, and

Japan and Norway have one title each. In 2023 Australia and New Zealand will host the competition, which will be the first time the Women's World Cup has ever been held in the Southern Hemisphere or hosted by two countries.

The first World Cup I ever played in with the Matildas was hosted by Germany in 2011. Our coach was Tom Sermanni and we had eight players under the age of twenty in the squad that year, including me. For a seventeen-year-old, playing in a World Cup was a hugely exciting experience.

Walking out onto the pitch, making my official World Cup debut, was when I was put on as a substitute in the 79th minute of our first group-stage match against Brazil. In that same tournament, I was a starter for our second group-stage match against Equatorial Guinea, which we won, 3–2. We then went on to win against Norway, 2–1, in our final group-stage match. After finishing in second place in our group, we advanced to the knockout stage where we were unfortunately defeated by Sweden, 3–1.

The whole experience was surreal and overwhelming in the best possible way.

When the next World Cup came along, four years later in Canada, I almost didn't make it into the squad. The year before, in December 2014, I was playing with Perth Glory in a match against Canberra United when I suffered a knee injury in the second half of the game.

My knee needed surgery, ruling me out of the rest of the 2014 W-League season. Being forced out of play for that long was a crushing blow, but having football taken away at that stage of my career was also a massive wake-up call and a total game-changer for me, personally. That was when I realised that I wasn't doing all I could to be the best player I could be. I'd always had a lot of natural ability and been able to keep up with the rest of my teammates at trainings and out on the pitch, but when I did my anterior cruciate ligament (ACL) I realised that I was nowhere near as fit as I should be and that I needed to lose weight. Also, it was hard watching my teammates heading out onto the pitch every week. I had chronic FOMO and hated being on the sidelines instead of out there on the field.

I had a revelation then. I suddenly realised just how much I loved football and that I wanted to keep playing it for as long as I could. More than anything else, I desperately wanted to be the best female football player in the world. Not being able to play opened my eyes to how much I had been taking the game, and being able to play it, for granted up until then. I promised myself that once I was recovered, I would never take it for granted ever again. Doing my knee like that and being out of play gave me the motivation I needed to knuckle down and work a lot harder than I had been up until that point, so in hindsight I'm glad the injury happened because it gave me the push I needed to take my skills and my game to the next level.

My dad and brother had always worn the number 4 on their jerseys when they were playing football, and for as long as I could remember I'd had a stubborn idea in my head that I should wear that number, too. But after my injury I had a revelation about that. Instead of complaining about not having the number I wanted, I was going to make the best of the number I had been given. Number 20 was going to be the Sam Kerr number. I was going to own number 20, making it mine and mine alone.

During that whole period, I worked harder than I ever had in my whole sporting life. My fitness coach, Aaron Holt, worked with me to help me recover after my surgery, and my coaches, rehab team and teammates all helped motivate and support me, too. I was so grateful to have them all around me during that time, encouraging me to get better and back on the pitch. I lost weight, got fitter and did everything my physio, doctors and coaches told me to do to get it back in top shape.

Finally, I was in good-enough shape to head off to Canada with the rest of the Matildas to play in the 2015 FIFA Women's World Cup with our coach, Alen Stajcic. I was the team's starting striker during our first group-stage match against the USA, which we lost, 3–1, but during our second group-stage match we defeated Nigeria, 2–0. That was also the match where Ugo Njoku elbowed me in the face, resulting in a three-game suspension for the Nigerian player. Luckily, I recovered quickly from that incident and went on to start in the final group-stage match against Sweden. That match was a draw, 1–1, and we finished second in our group.

'One to tell my kids about. Any time you break a record, especially for your country, it's an amazing feeling. Something like that is what I might look back on at the end of my career but right now I'm just happy to help the team.'

SAM KERR ON HER RECORD-BREAKING PERFORMANCE AT THE 2019 WORLD CUP

Advancing to the round of sixteen, we played Brazil and defeated them, 1–0, putting us in the quarterfinal match against Japan. At the end of the game against Brazil, their players were so furious we'd beaten them that they wouldn't shake our hands. I didn't care. The most important thing for us was about reaching this stage in a Women's World Cup for the first time ever. We were so proud of ourselves and how well we'd played. Unfortunately, we were defeated by Japan, 1–0, in the quarterfinal, and they then went on to win the Cup in the final against the USA. Despite our loss, I felt so honoured to have played alongside my brilliant teammates, and I had an amazing experience. Personally I was disappointed that I hadn't scored any goals in any of our World Cup games, but I would have my chance in the next World Cup in France in 2019.

In February 2019, I was named captain of the Australian National Women's Team for the World Cup, which was one of the greatest honours of my career. Our newly appointed head coach Ante Milicic gave me this amazing opportunity and huge honour, and I had big boots to fill. It was a lot of pressure to be given this role, but was also one that I felt ready and excited for.

During the Matildas first group-stage match in the tournament, we got an early lead against Italy when I finally scored my first-ever World Cup goal off a penalty kick rebound. It was a magnificent moment and I punched the corner flag as a nod to my hero, Tim Cahill, the all-time leading goal scorer for the Socceroos. We ultimately lost that game, 2–1 in stoppage time, but I'll never forget the feeling I had after scoring that first goal. We won our second group-stage match against Brazil, 3–2, and our next match was against Jamaica. It was an awesome match, and I was on a bit of a goal-scoring roll. The first two goals I scored were headers, drawing comparisons from the press between me and Tim Cahill, who is known for his header goals. Afterwards, when I was asked about them, I joked that I was 'coming for Tim's heading record'. I grew up watching Tim in awe of his header goals, which is why they are my favourite type of goals to score. It's an action that feels natural to me, which I reckon comes from my years of playing AFL. When I'm leaping up for a header, it's kind of the same feeling of getting air when going for a mark in Aussie Rules. I love it. It's like flying. But although I know it's a skill and strength I have, I am always working on it and trying to get better.

We won that game against Jamaica, 4–1, and I ended up scoring all four goals. On the night we won, I wasn't aware of how high the stakes were for us. With our win against Jamaica, we had pushed Brazil into third place, but that position wasn't going to be secured until the full-time whistle in each of the matches. Brazil were playing Italy, and another goal for either Brazil or Jamaica would have pushed us down to third, which would have been a much tougher draw. But our pre-match mantra had been to stay focused on our own game and to just keep on attacking at every opportunity, rather than change our tactics depending on where we were in the group standing.

So, while everyone else was stressing as they were waiting to see the final results that night, I didn't have a clue how important it was because I deliberately didn't ask what the score was in the other game until ours had finished. For us, it was all about focusing on ourselves. The last goal ended up sealing our position and so we were pretty happy about that. To top off the amazing experience, I was chuffed to be awarded the Player of the Match title afterwards.

The Matildas finished second in our group, which advanced us to the knockout stage where we were unfortunately defeated by Norway in a penalty shoot-out.

When it came to goal-scoring during the tournament, I ended up coming in second with five goals in total. Ellen White, Megan Rapinoe and Alex Morgan all notched up six goals each. But it was a huge honour to know that I was the first Australian footballer – male or female – to score a hat-trick at a World Cup tournament, and only the tenth footballer ever to score four goals. These kinds of stats are obviously fantastic, but of course I know that I'm only as good as the team around me, and that really the honour belongs to all of us, not just me.

'Sam is resilient, a natural goal scorer and she plays for the badge. I just love her attitude, especially in the box. She brings in her whole team behind her. A lot of kudos to the kid. I would pay to watch her.'

HUE MENZIES,
JAMAICA COACH

WOMEN'S WORLD CUP TRIVIA

DID YOU KNOW?

- The inaugural Women's World Cup was held in 1991 in China, 61 years after the first men's World Cup. The event was won by the USA.

- USA captain Kristine Lilly is the only woman, and one of only three players in history, to appear in 5 football world cups. Norwegian player Bente Nordby played in 1995, 1999, 2003 and 2007. In 1991 she was in the squad but did not play.

- The USA is the only country to win the competition four times (1991, 1999, 2015, 2019).

- The 2007 Women's World Cup is the only World Cup (for men or women) in which every competing team had played in a previous final tournament.

- In 2011, Japan became the first Asian team to win a FIFA World Cup (either men or women).

- Australian Ellyse Perry has appeared in both the ICC Women's Cricket World Cup (2009) and the FIFA Women's World Cup (2011).

- The 2015 FIFA Women's World Cup was the first to be played on artificial turf.

- The 2015 FIFA Women's World Cup featured the youngest coach in World Cup history: Ecuador's Vanessa Arauz, at 26 years old.

- Three countries have participated in the FIFA Women's World Cup without ever qualifying for the men's version: Taiwan, Thailand and Equatorial Guinea.
- US player, Christie Rampone, became the oldest player in Women's World Cup history in 2015 when she played at 40 years of age.
- Carli Lloyd of the USA became the first woman to score a hat-trick in a World Cup final in 2015.

'The World Cup in 2023 is going to be amazing. I think it's going to be the best World Cup ever, not just because Australia is hosting it, but because the quality in women's football has improved dramatically in the last four years.'

Sam Kerr

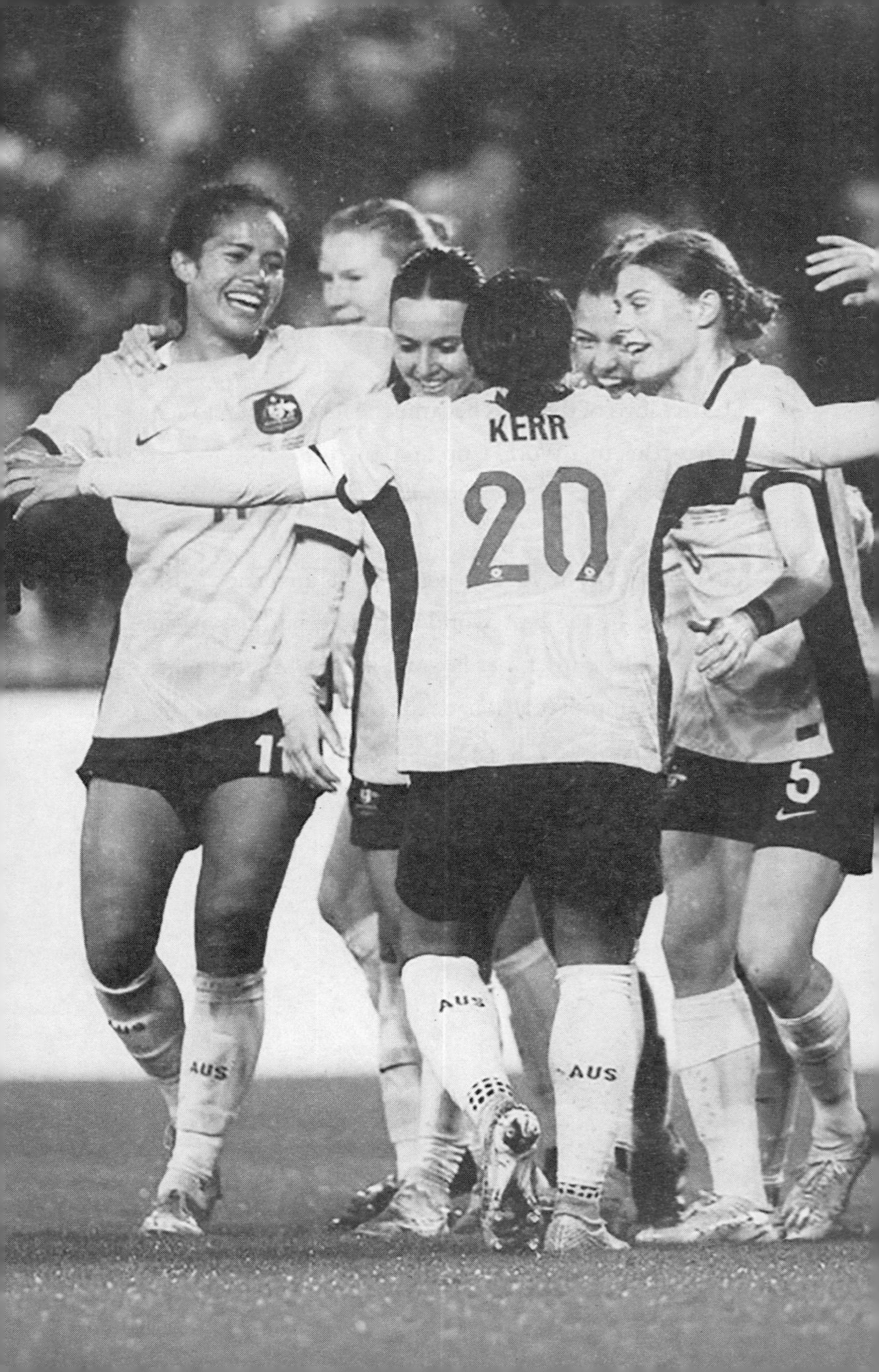
KERR
20
5
AUS
AUS
AUS

2023 WORLD CUP

In the lead-up to this year's World Cup, I'm training harder than ever, as well as preparing myself mentally. I'm also focusing on my nutrition, bonding with my team, trying to ignore any negativity or pressure, having enough rest and down time, and maintaining a positive mindset and attitude.

With the World Cup now only a few weeks away, this is what my training schedule and daily routine look like:

- Minimum eight hours sleep
- Morning coffee
- Train
- Recovery
- Relax

SLEEP

Sleep is very important to me, both before and after big games. I like to get a minimum of eight hours to make sure I'm completely rested and ready to go.

DIET AND NUTRITION

Nutrition is a huge part of my preparation before a game. I eat really clean; I do drink lots of coffee (good coffee) and mostly stick to boring meals to keep myself fit and in shape. Healthy eating makes me feel good. My favourite food to eat the night before a big competition is pasta. Carb loading is really important. I treat myself every now and then, but most of the time I take the healthy options when it comes to eating.

TRAINING SCHEDULE

In a game week, our training schedule will be four field sessions and one gym session. In my gym session I focus on leg workouts, resistance exercises using my body weight and bridges. On the field during training, we run through various tactical drills – either defensive play or counterattacks.

RELAX

I try and spend at least two to three hours a day relaxing my body to give it time to recover from all the training and playing I'm doing.

'The legacy we want to leave is that we inspire a nation. That we move the nation to believe in women's football and the Matildas. It's about getting people higher up to believe in the sport and getting money into football to allow girls to play and have the opportunity to get where they want to be. We have the participation, we have the love of the game, but we hope that the lasting legacy will be funding.'

SAM KERR

GAME DAY

My favourite song to listen to prior to competing changes all the time, but it's mostly Drake. To calm my butterflies before a game, I have a coffee and try to relax.

STRETCHING

This is so important before a big match. Stretching is key if you want to try and avoid being injured. It's also crucial to warm up your body this way before an intensive and very physical game. Before I do any training, I always stretch and relax my hamstrings, quads, groin, glutes and calves. I also use exercise bands to activate my leg muscles.

RECOVERY

When the game is over, I go back to the locker room and straight away have a small amount of protein and fruit to repair my muscles, feed my body and curb my hunger from all the running I've done in the past ninety minutes. I also drink lots to replenish the fluids I've lost during the game. After that, my routine includes taking an ice bath (which feels like torture during it but so good afterwards!) and having a massage treatment.

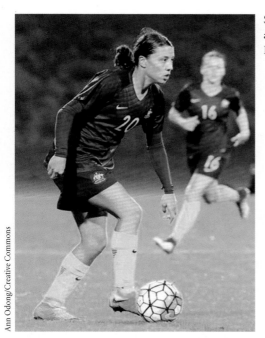

Sam plays with the Matildas at the 2017 Algarve Cup in Portugal.

Sam scores her first hat trick playing for Perth Glory in 2014.

Sam scores her first Olympic goal at the 2016 Olympic Games in Rio de Janeiro, Brazil.

The Matildas make Olympic history when they come fourth at the 2020 Olympic Games in Tokyo, Japan.

Sam Kerr's image is projected onto the Sydney Opera House on 25 June 2020, ahead of the announcement of which country would host the 2023 FIFA Women's World Cup.

Sam plays against Maren Mjelde of Norway during the 2019 FIFA Women's World Cup round of 16 football match between Norway and Australia in Nice, France.

Captain Sam Kerr celebrates with head coach Ante Milicic after beating Brazil at the 2019 FIFA Women's World Cup in France.

Christine Lynch 2020

The Matildas play at the AFC Women's Football Olympic Qualifiers where they won 6–0 against Thailand in the Campbelltown Sports Stadium in 2020.

Rachel Bach/By The White Line

Sam Kerr greeting and inspiring young fans.

Sam Kerr is congratulated by her teammates after scoring another goal. Teamwork is all about sharing the good times and the not-so-good times with each other.

Australia's Kyah Simon is embraced by teammates Katrina Gorry, left, and Sam Kerr as they celebrate Simon's goal against Brazil during the 2015 FIFA Women's World Cup quarterfinal in New Brunswick, Canada.

Sam Kerr celebrates scoring a goal for Chelsea Women's.

Sam Kerr became the first female footballer to feature on the cover of the hugely popular FIFA video game alongside French star Kylian Mbappé on the cover of FIFA 23 Ultimate Edition.

Sam celebrates her fourth goal in Chelsea Women's win against Vllaznia in the Champions League with her signature on-field backflip.

2023 WORLD CUP
STATS AND FACTS

For the first time since its inception, the Women's World Cup will have thirty-two teams competing instead of twenty-four. This, as well as the fact that more than a billion people tuned in to watch the 2019 Women's World Cup, is proof that women's football is becoming more popular every year all over the world.

TEAMS

- Argentina
- Australia
- Brazil
- Canada
- China
- Colombia
- Costa Rica
- Denmark
- England
- France
- Germany
- Haiti
- Italy
- Jamaica
- Japan
- Republic of Korea (South Korea)
- Morocco
- Netherlands
- New Zealand
- Nigeria
- Norway
- Panama
- Philippines
- Portugal
- Republic of Ireland
- South Africa
- Spain
- Sweden
- Switzerland
- USA
- Vietnam
- Zambia

PLAYERS TO WATCH . . . APART FROM SAM, OF COURSE!

ALEXIA PUTELLAS (SPAIN)

Alexia is captain of both the Spanish National team and Barcelona. She is a favourite of fans in Barcelona and is a two-time Ballon d'Or Féminin winner. She is currently recovering from an injury after tearing her anterior cruciate ligament (ACL) but is expected to be fit and healthy for the World Cup in July. A mural depicting Putellas as Superwoman over the slogan 'Follow your dreams' has been painted in a plaza of Barcelona. The artist wanted to inspire more young girls to become footballers.

ADA HEGERBERG (NORWAY)

Ada is a striker from Norway who is a Ballon d'Or Féminin winner and the leading female goalscorer in the Union of European Football Associations (UEFA) history. Ada refused to play in the 2019 World Cup based on her concerns that Norway's women's team was not being given the same opportunities as the men's football squad.

'I'm so proud that Australia is in a position where we're able to host a World Cup. We deserve it and I think we're going to show the world what an amazing country we have, and what a sporting country we have. I'm just so excited. I can't even imagine what it's going to be like and now the buzz is already starting. We can't wait to welcome everyone to Australia.'

SAM KERR

2023 WORLD CUP SCHEDULE

Group stage – Matchday 1 of 3			
New Zealand	20 July 23	Australia	20 July 23
Norway	5:00 pm	Republic of Ireland	8:00 pm
Nigeria	21 July 23	Philippines	21 July 23
Canada	12:30 pm	Switzerland	3:00 pm
Spain	21 July 23	USA	22 July 23
Costa Rica	5:30 pm	Vietnam	11:00 am
Zambia	22 July 23	England	22 July 23
Japan	5:00 pm	Haiti	7:30 pm
Denmark	22 July 23	Sweden	23 July 23
China	10:00 pm	South Africa	3:00 pm
Netherlands	23 July 23	France	23 July 23
Portugal	5:30 pm	Jamaica	8:00 pm
Italy	24 July 23	Germany	24 July 23
Argentina	4:00 pm	Morocco	6:30 pm
Brazil	24 July 23	Colombia	25 July 23
Panama	9:00 pm	South Korea	12:00 pm
Group stage – Matchday 2 of 3			
New Zealand	25 July 23	Switzerland	25 July 23
Philippines	3:30 pm	Norway	6:00 pm
Japan	26 July 23	Spain	26 July 23
Costa Rica	3:00 pm	Zambia	5:30 pm
Canada	26 July 23	USA	27 July 23
Republic of Ireland	10:00 pm	Netherlands	11:00 am
Portugal	27 July 23	Australia	27 July 23
Vietnam	5:30 pm	Nigeria	8:00 pm
Argentina	28 July 23	England	28 July 23
South Africa	10:00 am	Denmark	6:30 pm
China	28 July 23	Sweden	29 July 23
Haiti	9:00 pm	Italy	5:30 pm
France	29 July 23	Panama	29 July 23
Brazil	8:00 pm	Jamaica	10:30 pm
South Korea	30 July 23	Germany	30 July 23
Morocco	2:30 pm	Colombia	7:30 pm

Group stage – Matchday 3 of 3			
Norway Philippines	30 July 23 5:00 pm	Switzerland New Zealand	30 July 23 5:00 pm
Japan Spain	31 July 23 5:00 pm	Costa Rica Zambia	31 July 23 5:00 pm
Republic of Ireland Nigeria	31 July 23 8:00 pm	Canada Australia	31 July 23 8:00 pm
Vietnam Netherlands	1 Aug 23 5:00 pm	Portugal United States	1 Aug 23 5:00 pm
China England	1 Aug 23 9:00 pm	Haiti Denmark	1 Aug 23 9:00 pm
Argentina Sweden	2 Aug 23 5:00 pm	South Africa Italy	2 Aug 23 5:00 pm
Panama France	2 Aug 23 8:00 pm	Jamaica Brazil	2 Aug 23 8:00 pm
Morocco Colombia	3 Aug 23 8:00 pm	South Korea Germany	3 Aug 23 8:00 pm

GROUPS			
GROUP A New Zealand Norway Philippines Switzerland	**GROUP B** Australia Republic of Ireland Nigeria Canada	**GROUP C** Spain Costa Rica Zambia Japan	**GROUP D** England Haiti Denmark China
GROUP E USA Vietnam Netherlands Portugal	**GROUP F** France Jamaica Brazil Panama	**GROUP G** Sweden South Africa Italy Argentina	**GROUP H** Germany Morocco Colombia South Korea

WORLD CUP PREDICTOR

There will be 64 matches played over 31 days in nine different cities, from Auckland to Wellington and Adelaide to Sydney. The top two teams from each group advance to the knockout

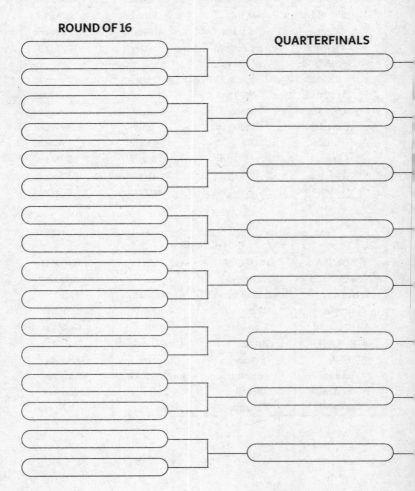

ROUND OF 16

QUARTERFINALS

stage, which starts with the round of 16. Once you know the results, fill in the chart and follow the teams as they advance to the quarterfinals, semifinals then on to the final.

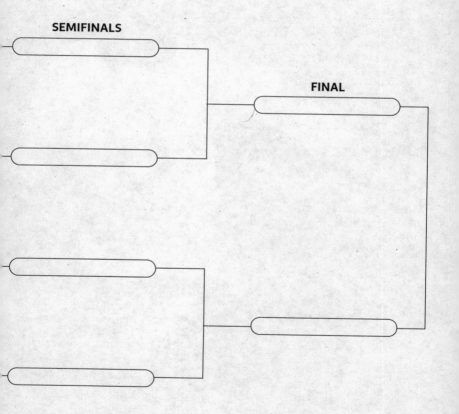

SAM'S STATS AND AWARDS

- **2006:** Starts playing football as a junior at Western Knights, Mosman Park.
- **2009:** Plays her first match for Perth Glory during the Women's League season.
- **2009:** First senior international cap in 2009 at 15 years of age.
- **2010–11:** Starts in all 10 matches and scored 3 goals for Perth Glory.
- **2012:** Joins Sydney Football Club.
- **2013:** Gets snapped up by Western New York Flash team for the USA's National Women's Soccer League. Scores 6 goals in 21 appearances.
- **2014:** Starts in all 20 matches for the Western New York Flash and is the team's top scorer with 9 goals.

- **2014:** Returns to Perth Glory and goes on to play for them in every Women's League season from 2014–15 to 2018–19 (scores 17 league goals in 13 appearances).
- **2015:** Traded to Sky Blue Football Club in New Jersey after the 2015 FIFA Women's World Cup. Scores 6 goals in 9 appearances.
- **2016:** Makes 9 appearances with Sky Blue and in the national team at the Rio Olympics.
- **2017:** Makes her mark on the National Women's Soccer League (NWSL) playing with Sky Blue. Scores 4 goals in the second half of a match against Seattle Reign.
- **2017:** Wins the NWSL Golden Boot and MVP award after a record 17 goals.
- **2018:** Is traded to the Chicago Red Stars and picks up the NWSL Player of the Month award for the third time in her career.
- **2019:** In the FIFA Women's World Cup, Sam is the first Australian player (male or female) to score a hat-trick at a World Cup tournament.
- **2019:** Sam and the Chicago Red Stars make their first appearance in the NWSL Championship.
- **2019:** Sam leaves the NWSL to sign a two-and-a-half-year contract with Chelsea.
- **2019:** Sam nets her 64th career goal in W-League, becoming the all-time leading scorer in that league as well.

- **2020:** Sam makes her debut for Chelsea against Reading and scores her first goal a fortnight later against Arsenal.

- **2021:** Plays in the 2020 Olympic Games in Tokyo and scores in the opening game against New Zealand. In the bronze medal match, she scores a goal to become the all-time top scorer for the Matildas, surpassing Lisa De Vanna.

- **2021:** Sam celebrates 100 caps and 48 goals with the Matildas.

- **2021:** Sam helps Chelsea to reach the UEFA Women's Champions League final for the first time, and wins 8 trophies, including back-to-back Women's Super League titles.

- **2022:** Sam is awarded the Order of Australia medal in recognition of her services to the sport of football.

- **2022:** Sam wins her 100th cap against the Republic of Ireland and returns to Australia to play two friendly matches against Brazil on home soil.

- **2022:** Sam plays in the AFC Women's Asian Cup in India where she scores 5 goals in Australia's opening match of the group stage against Indonesia, equaling and surpassing the Australian international goal-scoring record, among both male and female Australian internationals, previously set by Tim Cahill.

- **2023:** Sam wins the FA Women's Super League Player of the Year award for the second consecutive year.

'Me and Timmy [Cahill] have a lot of mutual respect. He's an idol of mine, so to break his record – and even be in the same sentence as him – I have to pinch myself. But although I enjoyed getting to that record, I'm actually glad it's done now so I can finally stop talking about it!'

Sam Kerr

MORE AMAZING SAM FACTS

- Sam Kerr has won the Golden Boot award in 3 different leagues.
- Wins the W-League Championship with Sydney FC in 2012–13.
- W-League Premiership with Perth Glory in 2014.
- Wins the 2013 NWSL Shield with the Western New York Flash.
- Sam is a four-time recipient of the PFA's Women's Footballer of the Year Award in 2013, 2017, 2018 and 2019.
- In 2013 and 2014, she is named International Player of the Year by the Football Media Association.
- First and only Aussie women's footballer to be shortlisted for the Ballon d'Or Féminin.
- In 2017 is the top goalscorer at the inaugural Tournament of Nations in the USA.
- In 2017 is named the AFC Women's Footballer of the Year.

- From 2017 to 2021 is named in the Top 10 of *The Guardian*'s 100 Best Female Footballers in the World, ranking 3rd, 2nd, 1st, 6th and 3rd, respectively.

- In 2017 and 2018, Sam was awarded the Julie Dolan Medal as the best player in Australia.

- In 2018 Kerr was named the 2018 Young Australian of the Year.

- In 2018, 2019 and 2022, Sam received the ESPY (Excellence in Sports Performance Yearly) Award for Best International Women's Football Player.

- In 2019 she won the ESPY Award for Best NWSL Soccer Player.

- In 2022 Kerr was awarded a Medal of the Order of Australia (OAM) as part of the Australia Day Honours, for her services to football. She was only the second female footballer to receive this honour, after Matildas' captain, Julie Dolan.

- In 2022 Sam was awarded the FWA Women's Footballer of the Year.

- In 2022 it was announced that Sam would feature on the cover of the FIFA 23 video game alongside Kylian Mbappé. It was the first time a female player has appeared on the global cover of the game franchise.

MORE Q & A WITH SAM

Q: What sports do you love other than the one in which you are already a professional?

A: I'm a big sport lover of tennis, netball, basketball, NFL and AFL. You name it, I love it!

Q: Would you ever go back to playing AFL?

A: Not a chance. There's been a lot of talk about me going back to AFL, but why would I go back to starting something new, starting at the bottom again, when we've spent so many years growing the Matildas brand? I feel like I owe this game so much. It's given me my life.

Q: What's your favourite part about playing at home?

A: My favourite part is playing in front of a home crowd and my family and friends.

Q: If you weren't playing football what would you be doing?

A: I would have liked to be a doctor.

Q: What are you favourite, dogs or cats?

A: Dogs (sorry to Helen, my cat).

Q: What's the best and hardest part about being captain of the Matildas?

A: The best part about being the captain is the amazing honour it is to get to lead the girls out every game. The hardest part of being the captain is that you can't always please everyone.

Q: If you were stuck on a desert island, which two Matildas and Cheslsa teammates would you take?

A: From the Matildas, I'd probably take Clare Polkinghorne, because she would keep me alive, and maybe Emily Van Egmond, because she would keep me entertained. And from Chelsea, I'd probably take Millie Bright, because once again she would keep me alive and would protect me, and Erin Cuthbert, because she would entertain me.

Q: What is your favourite potato chip?

A: Probably salt and vinegar crinkle cut, to be exact.

Q: What do you like on your ice cream?

A: I actually am really simple and just like plain ice cream with no toppings. But nuts, if anything. Hazelnuts especially.

Q: What's on your 'Pump up' playlist?

A: I actually like a bit of drum and bass, so a little bit of Sub Focus and Dimension.

Q: What's your favourite cheat meal?

A: A double cheeseburger.

Q: Do you prefer going to the beach or the mountains?

A: Definitely the beach.

'Don't just win.
Show the world
what's possible.'

SAM KERR

HOW WELL DO YOU KNOW YOUR WORLD CUPS?

Test your knowledge with the following questions:

- When was the first Men's World Cup played?
- Which country has won the most World Cups?
- Which is the only country to have played at every World Cup?
- What year did the Women's World Cup start?
- Which Aussie has appeared in both the Women's Cricket World Cup and the Football World Cup?
- How many teams played in the very first Men's World Cup?
- Which country has played in the least number of matches in the World Cup?
- What is the most common score in a World Cup finals match?

- Which two World Cup finals have been decided on penalties?
- Which is the smallest country (in terms of population) to reach the World Cup?
- Who is the only male player to score at five World Cups?

'There's definitely more to come from me. Everyone's trying to say twenty-nine is the peak age but people like Megan Rapinoe won FIFA's The Best award years after that, as did Carli Lloyd, and I know I still have more to give. I'm really excited about where I'm going in my career, where my national team is going and where my club is going. I feel I'm only just starting to play my best football and doing it at a consistent level. Hopefully people believe I have more to give – because I do.'

Sam Kerr

'Be the player the world can't stop.'

SAM KERR

SAM KERR QUIZ

1. What is Sam Kerr's birthdate?
   A. 10 September 1992
   B. 13 September 1992
   C. 10 September 1993
   D. 13 September 1993

2. What is Sam Kerr's middle name?
   A. March
   B. April
   C. May
   D. June

3. How tall is Sam Kerr?
   A. 1.47 m
   B. 1.57 m
   C. 1.67 m
   D. 1.77 m

4. How many siblings does Sam Kerr have?

    A. 1

    B. 2

    C. 3

    D. 4

5. What is Sam Kerr's dog's name?

    A: Billie

    B: Bear

    C: Sammy

    D: Tillie

6. What age did Sam Kerr make her international debut?

    A. 14

    B. 15

    C. 16

    D. 17

7. Which country does Sam Kerr play for?

    A. USA

    B. Canada

    C. England

    D. Australia

8. Which club does Sam Kerr play for?

    A. Arsenal

    B. Chelsea

    C. Southampton

    D. Barcelona

9. What position does Sam Kerr play?
   A. Midfield
   B. Defense
   C. Forward
   D. Spin bowler

10. As a child, which sport did Sam Kerr play before football?
   A. Rugby
   B. Aussie Rules football
   C. Hurling
   D. Cricket

11. What is Sam Kerr's way of celebrating goals?
   A. Backflip
   B. Forward roll
   C. Crawling
   D. Shouting and running

12. Before Chelsea, for which club did Sam Kerr play?
   A. Chicago Red Stars
   B. Reading FC
   C. Boston Red Socks
   D. Red Star Belgrade

13. As of 2022, Sam Kerr is the only female player to have been a top scorer in three continents.
   A. True
   B. False

14. What star sign is Sam?

    A. Leo

    B. Aries

    C. Sagittarius

    D. Virgo

15. What year did Sam Kerr pick up awards for Goal of the Year and Players' Player of the Year at the W-League?

    A. 2003

    B. 2006

    C. 2009

    D. 2012

DID YOU KNOW?

Sam Kerr was the Australian flag-bearer at King Charles III's coronation at Westminster Abbey. 'It's an amazing honour,' Sam said about being asked, 'but I wasn't sure if I could do it because we had a game on the next day. But Emma Hayes (the Chelsea manager) let me miss practice for it, which was very nice of her.'

Answers: 1(c), 2(c), 3(c), 4(c), 5(a), 6(b), 7(d), 8(b), 9(c), 10(b), 11(a), 12(a), 13(a), 14(d), 15(c)

'I don't just want to be a player that was good for a certain amount of years. I want to have a legacy.'

SAM KERR

SAM KERR'S LIFE IN PICTURES

Proud auntie Sam loves her family coming to watch her when she plays.

Family is all important to Sam. She spends as much time as she can with her mum, dad, brothers and nanna when she is at home.

Sam loves hanging out with her sister, nieces and nephews.

Sam with her partner Kristie Mews relaxing on Rottnest Island.

Sam tries to travel with Kristie whenever she can.

Sam loves making their training sessions fun.

Sam loves meeting her fans and hopes she can encourage more kids to want to play football.

Sam says it's important to have lots of jokes and laughter when you are training and competing.

Sam's family, including the little ones, are her greatest supporters.

Sam says teamwork is the most important thing for the Matildas. She believes that when you are part of a fantastic team, the players become much more than just teammates. They become your best friends.

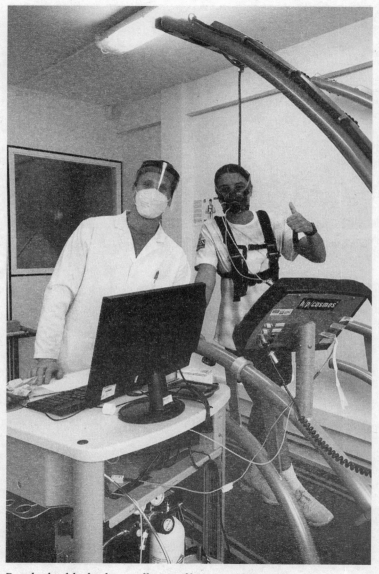

Regular health checks are all part of being an elite athlete.

Sam's mum and dad love travelling and try and watch her play in England whenever they can.

Training in England in freezing conditions took a bit of getting used to for Sam.

Sam signed with Chelsea Football Club at the end of 2019 and is the only female player to have scored 50 goals in the English Women's Super League, and is the top female scorer in three continents.

Sam helps to win another trophy for Chelsea.

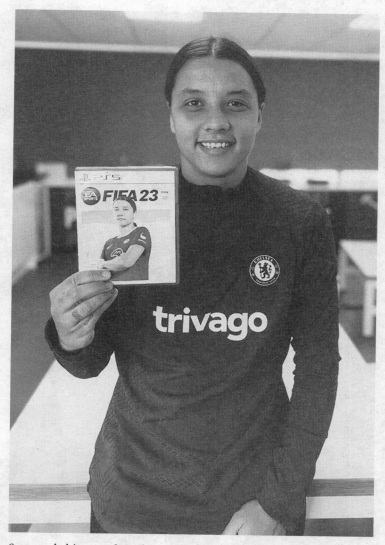

Sam made history when she was chosen to feature on the cover of FIFA 23. It was the first time a female player had ever featured on the cover.

Playing in tournaments was challenging during Covid.

CREDITS

SOURCES

Australian Associated Press, 'Sam Kerr admits challenging start to Chelsea career', The Guardian, 5 February 2020, https://www.theguardian.com/sport/2020/feb/05/sam-kerr-testing-start-to-chelsea-career

Bradley, Shannon. 'Matildas star Samantha Kerr's advice to young girls playing soccer', Sydney Morning Herald, 24 November 2017, https://www.smh.com.au/lifestyle/matildas-star-samantha-kerrs-advice-to-young-girls-playing-soccer-20171114-gzknrq.html

Brennan, Clare. 'Everything you need to know about Sam Kerr', Just Women's Sports, 16 December 2021, https://justwomenssports.com/reads/everything-you-need-to-know-about-sam-kerr/

Burns, Brielle. 'I don't like sport. Interviewing Sam Kerr gave me a completely different perspective', Mamamia, 11 November 2022, https://www.mamamia.com.au/sam-kerr-fifa-23/

Coca-cola Australia, 'Powerade's new ambassador Sam Kerr's top 3 tips to play like a pro', 7 November 2018, https://www.coca-colacompany.com/au/news/powerade-ambassador-sam-kerr-top-tips

Downing, Sam. 'How to train like an elite soccer player: Matildas stars reveal their workout and diet tricks', Nine News, Accessed: 9 May 2023, https://coach.nine.com.au/fitness/matildas-womens-football-training-diet/02a2822f-bf34-4a7b-8709-eac0625eabeb

Edwards, Harry. 'Sam Kerr proves her doubters wrong (again) as Chelsea complete domestic treble', Squawka, 6 December 2021, https://www.squawka.com/en/sam-kerr-chelsea-2021-fa-cup-final-arsenal-domestic-treble/

FIFA, 'Kerr: The World Cup buzz is already starting', Accessed: 9 May 2023, https://www.fifa.com/fifaplus/en/articles/kerr-the-world-cup-buzz-is-already-starting

Giampetro, Julia. 'Aussie footballer Sam Kerr on living out her sports dream', Amodrn, 21 February, 2018, https://amodrn.com/footballer-sam-kerr-kicking-goals/

Gilby, Ben. 'Sam Kerr: "We wants to inspire a nation"', Impetus Football, 6 April 2023, https://impetusfootball.org/2023/04/06/sam-kerr-we-want-to-inspire-a-nation/

Hall, Matthew. 'Sam Kerr: 'There are no hierarchies, no cliques . . . we are fit and we are fast', The Guardian, 24 August 2017, https://www.theguardian.com/football/2017/aug/24/sam-kerr-when-the-goals-come-you-have-more-fun-its-a-ripple-effect

Humphreys, Jessy Parker. 'Sam Kerr's "rollercoaster" career: "I came to England a bit too much of a star"', Optus Sport, 26 March 2023, https://sport.optus.com.au/news/matildas/os49477/sam-kerr-interview-2022-fifa-23-chelsea-matildas-australia

Price, Julian. 'Exclusive: Aussie football star Sam Kerr on making the cover of FIFA 23 "It's like a dream come true"', Nine News, 23 July 2022, https://www.9news.com.au/technology/exclusive-sam-kerr-speaksto-9news-about-on-her-fifa-23-cover/369be29d-015d-43b1-a1da-09dc25b3947d

Rayson, Zac. '"Everyone only sees 90 minutes": Kerr reveals she played CL match with Covid-19', Fox Sports, 6 March 2022, https://www.foxsports.com.au/football/matildas/chelsea-2022-news-sam-kerr-matildas-wsl-cup-final-champions-league-chelsea-vs-wolfsburg/news-story/29e7466f806265202e74505235c40bbd

Rayson, Zac. 'Exclusive: Kerr opens up on Matildas' "really crappy" Cup nightmare', Fox Sports, 7 March 2022, https://www.foxsports.com.au/football/matildas/exclusive-kerr-opensup-on-matildas-really-crappy-cup-nightmare/news-story/729a41078c637999299bcc74fd534260

Shaveta, 'Quiz: How well do you know about Sam Kerr?' ProProfs, 25 September 2022, https://www.proprofs.com/quiz-school/quizzes/sam-kerr-quiz

Smith, Peter. 'High-flying Kerr soars to new Aussie landmark', FIFA, 18 June 2019, https://www.fifa.com/tournaments/womens/womensworldcup/france2019/news/high-flying-kerr-soars-to-new-aussie-landmark

ABOUT SAM KERR

Sam Kerr is the captain of the Australian women's national football team – the Matildas – and a leading goal scorer for Chelsea in the English FA Women's Super League. She burst onto the W-League scene as a 15 year old playing with Perth Glory. In 2016, she played for the Matildas at the Olympics in Brazil, and she was the top goal scorer in the 2017 Tournament of Nations. Since joining Chelsea in 2019, Sam has positioned herself as one of the best female strikers in the world. She was named 2018 Young Australian of the Year. In 2021, Sam became the Matildas' all-time top goal scorer at the Tokyo Olympics, and she is currently preparing for the FIFA Women's World Cup to be held in Australia and New Zealand in July and August 2023.

ABOUT FIONA HARRIS

Fiona Harris is an Australian actor and author who has written numerous children's book series including the *Super Moopers*, *Trolls* and *Miraculous*. She is the author of the five Sam Kerr *Kicking Goals* books. Fiona has also written a picture book with AFL star Marcus Bontompelli and is the author of two adult fiction books, *The Drop-off* and *The Pick-up*, both adapted from her internationally award-winning comedy web series, *The Drop Off*. Fiona has co-written and starred in TV sketch comedy shows including *SkitHouse* (Channel 10), *Flipside* (ABC TV) and *Comedy Inc – The Late Shift* (Channel 9) and was head scriptwriter on ABC3 TV's *Prank Patrol*. For more information on Fiona Harris, please visit fionaharris.com.